TRANSFORMED TEMPERAMENTS

TRANSFORMED TEMPERAMENTS

Tim LaHaye

author of

Spirit-Controlled Temperament
How to Be Happy Though Married

TYNDALE HOUSE PUBLISHERS
Wheaton, Illinois
Coverdale House Publishers Ltd., London, England

Library of Congress Catalog Card Number
77-152120. SBN 8423-7305-5, Cloth; 8423-
7306-3 Paper. Copyright © 1971 by Tyndale
House Publishers, Wheaton, Illinois 60187. All
rights reserved. Second printing, June 1971.
Printed in the United States of America.

CONTENTS

FOREWORD

The response to my first book on temperament, *Spirit-Controlled Temperament,* has both amazed and inspired me. The first paperback edition of one thousand copies was more than our congregation could use, but then the Campus Crusade for Christ bookstore in San Bernardino began selling it and two more printings were needed soon. The sales manager of Tyndale House Publishers read it just at the time I began praying that God would send us a publisher — my children were getting tired of collating, binding, and packaging their father's books in the garage!

I commented to my wife when she dropped me off at the San Diego Airport en route to a speaking engagement in Chicago: "I hope the Lord reveals his will to us on this trip about the future of *Spirit-Controlled Temperament.*" That night I met Bob Hawkins, from Tyndale House. After my speaking engagement he invited me out for dinner and informed me that he had read my book and felt it should be published nationally. I couldn't have agreed with him more — if not for the reading public, at least for my exhausted family.

Since that time we have all been amazed at the way God has used the book. Letters have come from many parts of the world — from missionaries, pastors, counselors, and laymen

— and several readers reported they found Christ as Savior through the books. To date it has been translated into Spanish, Japanese, and Russian. Three missionary societies have used it in training their candidates for the field. Churches have used it for study groups, Sunday school classes, and youth meetings. At this writing, more than 125,000 copies have been published. Needless to say, this has been most encouraging. I do not claim to have originated the concept of the four temperaments. My contribution comes in applying these time-honored classifications so every individual can examine himself, analyze both his strengths and weaknesses, and then seek the Holy Spirit's cure for those tendencies that keep him from being usable by God.

This new book, *Transformed Temperaments,* is the result of additional research into the subject and further counseling with people in trouble. Its inspiration came when I found a transformation of temperament in the lives of several Bible characters which I expect to find in Spirit-filled Christians today. It should be remembered that this transformation is not dependent on knowing the four temperaments, but on being filled with the Spirit. The Bible personalities we will meet were transformed before the temperament theory was formed. Our hope is in God's promise: "Therefore if any man be in Christ, he is a new creature: old things are passed away; behold, all things are become new" (2 Corinthians 5:17).

1

THE BIRTH OF "FOUR TEMPERAMENTS"

Hippocrates (460-370 B.C.) is often called the father of medicine; certainly he was the giant of the Greek medical world. He interests us for two reasons: (1) he is generally credited with making psychiatric problems a concern of medicine, and (2) he recognized temperamental differences in people and offered a theory to account for these differences. E. Baughman and George Welsh evaluated his contribution this way:

"The ancient world was aware of gross abnormalities in behavior, but it usually attributed them to the intervention of the gods and so failed to study them objectively. Hippocrates, however, opposed supernaturalism, supported a biological orientation, and thus developed an empirical approach to psychopathology. Perhaps his greatest strength lay in his acuteness of observation and his ability to record his observations and insights scientifically. Indeed, many of his descriptions of psychopathological phenomena ring true to today's clinician. Hippocrates, then, marked the beginning of a careful observational approach to abnormal personality, an approach that would one day be applied to normal personality.

"Hippocrates' interest in temperamental characteristics is noteworthy, especially considering the relative neglect of this important problem in today's psychological world. As a result

of his observations, Hippocrates distinguished four temperaments: the sanguine, the melancholic, the choleric, and the
phlegmatic. Which temperament a person possessed depended,
according to Hippocrates, on the 'humors' of his body: blood,
black bile, yellow bile, and phlegm. Thus Hippocrates began
with observed differences in behavior and went on to formu-
late a theory to explain these differences. Essentially the theory
was biochemical, but even though the substance of the theory
has vanished, its form remains with us. Today, however, instead of 'humors' we talk about hormones and other biochemical substances that may induce or affect the behavior we observe."[1]

The Romans did little in the way of creative intellectual-
ism, but seemed content to perpetuate the concepts of the
Greeks. A century and a half after the Roman Emperor Con-
stantine made Christianity the state religion in A.D. 312, the
empire crumbled into the "Dark Ages." Consequently, few al-
ternatives to Hippocrates' concept were offered until the nineteenth century. So little was done in personality studies that
when Galen revived the concept in the seventeenth century,
one modern writer, H. J. Eysenck,[2] attributed it to Galen instead of Hippocrates.

The German philosopher Immanuel Kant was probably most
influential in popularizing the four temperaments throughout
Europe. Although incomplete, Kant's description of the four
temperaments in 1798 was interesting. "The sanguine person
is carefree and full of hope; attributes great importance to
whatever he may be dealing with at the moment, but may
have forgotten all about it the next. He means to keep his
promises but fails to do so because he never considered deeply
enough to help others, but is a bad debtor and constantly asks
for time to pay. He is very sociable, given to pranks, contented,
does not take anything very seriously, and has many, many

[1]E. Earl Baughman and George Schalager Welsh, *Personality: A Behavioral Science* (New York: Prentice-Hall, 1962), p. 57. Used by
permission.
[2]H. J. Eysenck, *Fact and Fiction in Psychology* (Baltimore: Penguin
Books, 1965), p. 55. Used by permission.

friends. He is not vicious but difficult to convert from his sins; he may repent but this contrition (which never becomes a feeling of guilt) is soon forgotten. He is easily fatigued and bored by work but is constantly engaged in mere games — these carry with them constant change, and persistence is not his forte.

"People tending towards melancholia attribute great importance to everything that concerns them. They discover everywhere cause for anxiety and notice first of all the difficulties in a situation, in contradistinction to the sanguine person.

"He does not make promises easily because he insists on keeping his word, but has to consider whether he will be able to do so. All this is not because of moral considerations but because interaction with others makes him worried, suspicious, and thoughtful. It is for this reason that happiness escapes him.

"The choleric person is said to be hot-headed, is quickly roused, but easily calmed down if his opponent gives in; he is annoyed without lasting hatred. Activity is quick but not persistent. He is busy but does not like to be in business precisely because he is not persistent; he prefers to give orders but does not want to be bothered with carrying them out. He loves open recognition and wants to be publicly praised. He loves appearances, pomp and formality; he is full of pride and self-love. He is miserly; polite but with ceremony; he suffers most through the refusal of others to fall in with his pretensions. In one word, the choleric temperament is the least happy because it is most likely to call forth opposition to itself.

"Phlegma means lack of emotion, not laziness; it implies a tendency to be moved neither quickly nor easily but persistently. Such a person warms up slowly but he retains the warmth longer. He acts on principle not by instinct; his happy temperament may supply the lack of sagacity and wisdom. He is reasonable in his dealing with other people and usually gets his way by persisting in his objectives while appearing to give way to others."[3]

---

[3]Ibid., pp. 56-57.

Toward the close of the nineteenth century the study of human behavior received new impetus with the birth of the science of psychology. "University departments look back to the founding of Wundt's Laboratory of Experimental Psychology at Leipzig University in 1879 as the effective beginning of their discipline."[4] Dr. W. Wundt was probably influenced by Kant, for he too held to the four-temperament theory of human behavior. He performed exhaustive experiments trying to relate these temperaments to body structure, which led to the establishment of constitutional psychology, or attributing man's traits to his body structure. This concept, which has many followers, finally reduced the number of types to three. Some of the more recent students of this school have reduced the number to two, which tends to follow the much popularized classification of introvert-extrovert.

A devastating blow to the four-temperaments theory was dealt by Sigmund Freud around the turn of the century. His research and theorizing in psychoanalysis had an electrifying effect on the study of personality. "By implementing a completely deterministic point of view . . ."[5] Freud and his followers reflected their obsession with the idea that man's environment determined his behavior.

This idea, which is diametrically opposed to Christian theology, seriously undermined Western society. Instead of making man feel responsible for his own behavior, it gives him a scapegoat to blame for his bad behavior. If he steals, behaviorists tend to blame society because he lacks the things he needs. If he is poor, they blame society for not giving him a vocation. This behavioral concept has not only weakened man's innate sense of responsibility, it has discredited the helpful theory of the four temperaments. But if it can be established that man inherits certain temperament traits at birth, environmental theory will collapse.

During the first half of the twentieth century, most Chris-

[4]Bernard Notcutt, *Psychology of Personality* (New York: Philosophical Library, 1953), p. 7.
[5]Baughman and Welsh; Op. cit., p. 77.

tians seemed to suffer from an intellectual inferiority complex. The intellectual community loudly propagandized the theory of evolution as a "fact." Psychiatry and psychology mounted the academic throne where intellectuals bowed. Some, claiming to speak in the name of "science," ridiculed the Bible, the deity of Christ, sin, guilt, and a personal God. Many Christians attempted to adapt biblical concepts to the evolutionary concepts of "modern science." This compromise helped produce theological liberalism, modernism, neo-orthodoxy, and a crippled Church. Many Christians remained faithful to God and the Bible during those trying years but were strangely silent. A valiant few were prepared and willing to take on the intellectuals in open debate.

Today the tide is turning. The theory of evolution, a prominent foundation stone in the science of psychiatry and psychology, is cracking under steady scrutiny of scientists. Many psychiatrists and psychologists are disenchanted with Freudian psychology and behaviorism. A half century of observation confirms the skill of Freudians to diagnose personality problems, but raises questions about their ability to heal the sick. A new breed of psychiatrists is taking issue with some of the old ideas and experimenting with other theories. Some are even emphasizing the responsibility of man for his behavior, as the Bible teaches.*

During the first half of this century, only two Christian writers appear to have written about the four temperaments. Both were Europeans, but their works were distributed widely in the United States.

A great English preacher and theologian, Alexander Whyte (1836-1921), produced a brief work on the four temperaments. It is included in his *Treasury of Alexander Whyte*, published by Baker. No one can doubt after reading his masterful *Bible Characters* (Zondervan), that he was a student of the temperaments.

The most significant work on the four temperaments which

---

*See William Glasser's book, *Reality Therapy*, Harper & Row, 1965.

I know about is *Temperament and the Christian Faith,* by O. Hallesby. First published in Norwegian, it was translated into English and published by Augsburg Publishing House in 1962. Dr. Hallesby presented the four temperaments in vivid detail. His purpose was to help counselors recognize and relate to the four types of temperament. He also suggested possible remedies for problems that characterize each temperament.

My book *Spirit-Controlled Temperament* was inspired through the reading of this book. As a pastor-counselor I received many profitable insights from Dr. Hallesby, but I agonized over the hopeless condition in which he "left" the person with melancholy temperament. I thought, "If I were a Melancholy, I believe I would go out and shoot myself after reading this." But I knew there is plenty of hope for the melancholy temperament — or any temperament — in the power of Jesus Christ. It was then that God opened my eyes to the ministry of the Holy Spirit in the emotional life of the believer. I started to develop the concept that there is a divine strength for every human weakness through the filling of the Holy Spirit. After discussing the concept with hundreds of people and counseling many others, I am more convinced than ever that the nine characteristics of the Spirit-filled life, as described in Galatians 5:22-23, contain a strength for every weakness of the four temperaments: "The fruit of the Spirit is love, joy, peace, longsuffering, gentleness, goodness, faith, meekness, self-control; against such there is no law."

2

THE BLIGHT OF FREUDIANISM

Reader response to *Spirit-Controlled Temperament* has been fascinating to see. All human beings are vitally interested in what "makes them tick," which is why psychology is a favorite subject among college students. The four-temperaments explanation of "why you act the way you do" seems to make sense to people immediately. Housewives, college students, ministers, professional men, and people from all other walks of life can easily see themselves in one of the temperaments.

We began to hear of counselors, ministers, and psychologists who recommended the book to their clients. A nationally known Christian psychologist has recommended it all across the country. Several psychology teachers in Christian colleges have used it in their courses, and I have been asked to address many such classes.

The reaction of non-Christian psychologists and psychiatrists has been less than enthusiastic, but their rejection was expected. In the first place, the concept of four temperaments is not compatible with humanistic ideas; and, second, if psychiatrists do not believe in God, they instantly reject the power of the Holy Spirit as a cure for man's weaknesses.

Such thinking strongly influences reaction to the four temperaments. I spoke to almost one thousand students from colleges and universities across the country in a two-week seminar. The first session was an in-depth presentation of the four temperaments. Several young people were waiting for me, armed with questions, as soon as I was through. Almost all of them were "psych majors." Their main objection was, "You make it too simple" or "Your answers are simplistic."

Their response was understandable. They were absorbed in the process of learning the complex solutions to today's problems as our educators see them — not because the answers to man's problems are so complex, but because the molders of today's college curricula have rejected the Bible and God's plain cures for man's problems. Consequently, they are left with very involved solutions. The sad thing is that time does not seem to validate their solutions, and frustration sends them in search of another complex answer.

It is time for someone to point out that psychology and psychiatry are primarily based on atheistic humanism. Darwinism and Freudianism have shaped the thinking of the secular world until it builds most of its mental structure on two premises: there is no God, and man is a biological accident; man is supreme, and is sufficient to solve his problems. In philosophy studies I learned that "the validity of a conclusion is dependent on the accuracy of its premises." Since there actually is a God, the humanists' main premise is wrong; therefore we cannot expect their conclusions to be valid.

Much of the world today worships before the shrine of psychology and psychiatry. Since man must have a source of authority to lend credence to what he says, today's secularists usually quote some eminent psychologist. The fact that these authorities often contradict one another is usually not mentioned.

Do not misunderstand; I am not trying to ridicule sincere scholars. But I am calling attention to the danger of Christians being taken in by the "wisdom of the world." We need to recognize that "the wisdom of the world is foolishness with God" (1 Corinthians 1:18). The fact that men have doctoral degrees does not mean they are right. A roll call of the great philosophers of the world will show how each brilliant scholar disagreed with the great philosophers before him. A study of philosophy is frequently confusing because it is so contradictory. Experience and new knowledge have discredited the great philosophers. Christians, on the other hand, have one sure test for the accuracy of man's premises and conclusions: the Word of God! Man is right or wrong, depending on whether he agrees or disagrees with the Bible.

One senior "psych major" approached me after my final seminar and said, "I have to confess that I felt tremendous resistance against you after your first talk. You contradicted many things I have been taught, but as I listened, I came to realize that the Bible really does have the answer to man's problems! Thanks for coming here. You've been a blessing in my life." I hope this young lady and many others learned that there is nothing wrong with studying and using the valid principles of psychology and psychiatry or any other science as long as we validate them by the Word of God.

When I spoke at a couples' conference at beautiful Forest Home, high in the San Bernardino mountains, a psychologist attended all seven sessions. Because he was expressionless most of the time, I was dying with curiosity to know his reaction. Finally I got a chance to chat with him during the last meal together. He told me that he had been a counselor for almost twenty-five years. A few months previously he had received Christ as his personal Lord and Savior. Gradually he was becoming disenchanted with his techniques and the advice he had been giving for years. He had come to the conference to see if someone else had some better ideas. He concluded: "I am returning home with two clear impressions — the Bible has the answers to man's problems, and they really are quite simple."

The four temperaments seem to appeal to Christians because they are so compatible with many scriptural concepts. Just as the Bible teaches that all men have a sinful nature, the temperaments teach that all men have weaknesses. The Bible teaches that man has a besetting sin, and the temperaments highlight it. The Bible says man has "an old nature" which is the "flesh" or "corruptible flesh." Temperament is made up of inborn traits, some of which are weaknesses. The four-temperament classification is not categorically taught in the Bible, but our four biographical studies of Bible personalities will show temperamental strengths and weaknesses. The Bible shows that power over weaknesses is possible only when one receives Jesus Christ personally as Lord and Savior and yields one's self completely to his Spirit.

A psychologist friend informed me that there are twelve or thirteen theories of personality. The four-temperaments theory is probably the oldest, and many Christians consider it the best. It is not perfect — no concept of man is. It does, however, help the average person to examine himself by a process that has been systematized and improved through the centuries. It will not answer all your questions about yourself, but it will provide more answers than any other. As you study it, pause to thank God that you have access to a source of power that can change your life and make you the kind of person both you and God want you to be.

3

USE AND ABUSE OF THE TOOL

The four-temperaments theory is a valuable instrument for understanding yourself. But like any tool, it can be misused. Occasionally I meet people who have misused the concept and done a great disservice to themselves and others. The misuse usually occurs in the following ways.

Some casual observers of personality have externalized the concept, applying it indiscriminately to people they meet. And not being content just to think about it, they unceremoniously inform people what temperament they are, and outline their characteristic weaknesses. I have seen people rebuff their associates by naming their unfavorable temperament traits, exposing their weaknesses, and even humiliating them. This is dangerous. As psychologist Dr. Henry Brandt comments, "There is no nakedness comparable to psychological nakedness."

Human nature induces us to protect ourselves not just physically but psychologically. The individual who deliberately holds himself up for public ridicule is revealing a warped sense of emotional self-preservation. I suspect that such people use the exposure of lesser weaknesses as a shield for more severe but secret ones.

No Spirit-filled Christian would invade another person's privacy and expose him to psychological ridicule. It may be funny and it may spark humorous repartee at a gathering, but it may also be cruel and harmful. Anything that is not kind is not loving, and the Bible tells us to "speak the truth in love" (Ephesians 4:5). Since the indwelling Holy Spirit causes Christians to "love the brethren," we will grant them the emotional protection we cherish for ourselves.

Even when temperament analysis of others is not made public, it can be a harmful habit. A young woman revealed to me that she had rejected the friendship of a prospective suitor because she considered him an undesirable combination of temperaments. There is no such combination! No temperament is "better" than another, and temperament does not guarantee certain actions. An employer might reject a capable worker by jumping to a false conclusion about his temperament, and neither the young woman nor the employer has allowed for the transforming influence of the Holy Spirit.

The theory of the four temperaments is only a therapeutic tool. Whether used on others or on one's self, it should always be used gently, generally, and constructively. Here is a good rule to follow: don't analyze a person's temperament unless it will help you relate better to him, and don't tell a person his temperament unless he asks.

Another damaging use of the temperaments theory is to use it as an excuse for your behavior. Frequently people tell me, "The reason I do that is because I am a — temperament and can't help myself." That is self-deceit inspired by the devil. In addition, it is disbelief in God! Philippians 4:13 is either true or false: "I can do all things through Christ which strengtheneth me." If it is false, we cannot depend upon the Word of God. But since the Bible is true, God does supply all our need. Temperament may explain our behavior, but it never excuses it! Yet it is amazing how many people use it in that way. Consider the following statements made in the counseling room.

Mr. Sanguine, after an extramarital affair almost ruined his home, admitted, "I know I shouldn't have done it, but I'm a Sanguine and tend to be weak when exposed to sexual temptations." That was a cowardly way of saying: "It's God's fault — he made me this way!" Mr. Choleric, after being told that his angry outbursts had destroyed his unusual potential as a Bible teacher and Christian worker, announced: "I am a striker; I've always been a striker. When people cross me I tell them off!" That retort is characteristically choleric, but not the response of a Spirit-controlled Choleric.

Mrs. Melancholy came in for counseling after her husband left her and their three children. There was no other woman in his life — he simply felt compelled to leave. In parting he observed, "Since nothing I do ever pleases you, I've decided to get out of your life and let you find someone that doesn't have all my faults!" Through her tears this woman admitted, "I love my husband and I didn't mean to find fault with him all the time, but I'm a perfectionist and he is very careless. I feel that it's just as bad to think a thing as to say it, so I always told him when he was wrong — I just couldn't help it." A rather high price to pay for indulging in a selfish fixation, wouldn't you say?

Mr. Phlegmatic, whose desperate wife finally induced him to come for counseling, admitted that he had built a silent sound chamber for his psyche and crawled into it whenever his wife was around. Moderately friendly to others, at home he was the original "stone face." His outgoing wife found this intolerable. His response: "I'm an easygoing person that doesn't like turmoil and bickering. Rather than get into a feud, I just remain silent." This is a good way to induce ulcers not only in a mate, but in the Phlegmatic. Escape from reality behind a self-imposed wall of silence is not compatible with a father's role of leadership in the home.

These are examples of excuses used to justify self-centered behavior. Little or no cure can be effected until a person is willing to acknowledge that he has a problem. Instead of blaming one's temperament for aberrant behavior, the individual must recognize his natural weaknesses and let the Holy Spirit change them. Behavior does not reflect only temperament, but more significantly one's habit patterns. Temperament starts us out on a pattern of behavior; habit perpetuates and broadens it. A Christian is not a slave to habit! Habits — even life-long ones — can be changed by the divine Source of power within the Christian.

Discern your temperament

The best use of the temperament concept is possible only when you accurately discern your own temperament. For a complete study of the four temperaments see my book *Spirit-Controlled Temperament* (Tyndale House Publishers).

After carefully examining the temperament chart here, you may find your dominant temperament (or temperaments) by making a list of the traits that stand out in your life. Name your strengths first because it is easier to be objective about your strengths than your weaknesses. Once you have determined your strengths, find the corresponding weaknesses on the wheel. Many people are prone to change their minds when they examine the weaknesses, but it is best to resist this temptation and realistically face your shortcomings.

There are several factors to keep in mind when trying to discern your temperament. The most important is that *no one is characterized by just one temperament.* Since our parents and even our grandparents contribute to our makeup, everyone is a blend of at least two and sometimes three temperaments. The failure of Immanuel Kant and his European followers to allow for this fact, along with the advent of Freudian psychoanalysis, caused the concept to fall into disrepute. Kant's arbitrary insistence that everyone fit into one or the other of these four temperaments did not stand up under close scrutiny.

Everyone I have ever counseled has revealed traits of more than one temperament. However, one temperament will usually be more prominent than the other. For example, a Sanguine-Choleric may be 60 percent Sanguine and 40 percent Choleric. A Melancholy-Choleric may be 70 percent Melancholy and 30 percent Choleric. It is even possible that a person may be 50 percent Phlegmatic, 30 percent Sanguine and 20 percent Melancholy. I have had no success in trying to estab-

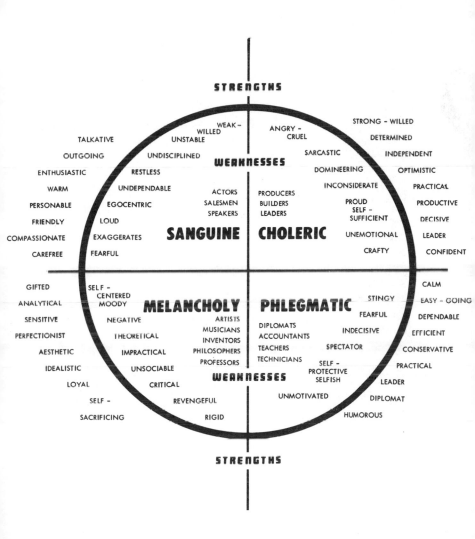

lish amounts or percentages of temperament, but the more dominant one temperament is, the easier it is to diagnose the personality. Sometimes it is impossible to determine the secondary temperament. Naturally, a person with two prominent temperaments or a combination of three temperaments would be difficult to diagnose.

A compensating reality for a person whose blend of temperaments makes analysis difficult is that he will not be extreme in any direction. If his strengths are not too apparent, neither will be his weaknesses. Therefore, there is no need for him to be frustrated because he lacks distinctive temperament traits. Such a person is perfectly normal, although in my experience quite rare.

Spiritual maturity

One factor commonly overlooked by Christians trying to analyze their temperaments is the modifying or maturing work already accomplished by the Holy Spirit. Temperament is based on the raw material with which we were born. Consequently the more spiritually mature a Christian is, the more difficult it is to diagnose the basic temperament. It is helpful, therefore, to examine the psychic raw material as it was before the Holy Spirit began his work.

When I went to a Midwest church for a family life and prophecy conference, the man in charge met me at the plane. At seventy-two he was the sweetest, most gracious, Spirit-filled Christian gentleman I had ever met. During the week I discovered that as president of one of the largest furniture companies in the world, he was unusually successful. The more I learned about him, the more confused I became. As a rule, phlegmatic men don't buy a bankrupt company in the middle of the depression and build it into a dynamic enterprise. That is something a Choleric would do. As I talked with his friends, the story gradually unfolded.

In his early days he was a typical, fire-eating Choleric with some melancholic tendencies. He worked night and day, organized, innovated, and produced where others had failed. In the mid-'30s he became a Christian. Quite by accident he began teaching Bible one night to a couple that had recently become Christians. The Bible study soon became a class, and then a special night had to be established. Eventually he was teaching three classes a week. Today there are two strong churches that grew out of these classes. But the change in him was equally exciting. As "the Word dwelt in him richly," the Holy Spirit molded his choleric temperament until he became a modern example of Spirit-controlled temperament. If you observe him carefully, you can see the choleric strengths of good organization and promotion ability, hard-driving, purposeful Christian work and creative optimism, even at seventy-two. Totally lacking are the anger, bitterness, resentment, cruelty, and other forms of choleric flesh. This man knew nothing about temperament, but he did know what it was to be filled with the Holy Spirit. So it isn't essential to know the principles of temperament to be modified by the Holy Spirit, but such principles will point up the greatest areas of weaknesses in our lives so we can speed up the process of modification.

Another factor to be considered when diagnosing your temperament is age. Most temperaments are easiest to discern between fifteen and thirty-five. From that point on, generally speaking, people have a tendency to become less pronounced in all their actions, unless habits, experiences, or other pressures accentuate them.

A person's physical condition will also affect the expressions of his temperament. High blood pressure can make an ordinarily sedate person appear more active than his temperament directs. Low blood pressure would tend to make a Sanguine or Choleric appear less intense than others. Some people have physiological structures that create nervous tensions — this will affect the expressions of their temperaments.

Sometimes childhood training forms early impressions and habits that make the secondary temperament seem dormant. When set free from these inhibitions by the Holy Spirit, the personality will show a marked change. My loving wife is an example.

She was raised in a rather strict environment and, during the early years of our marriage, was dominated a good deal by fear. If I had diagnosed her temperament at that time, I would have considered her about 70 percent Phlegmatic and 30 percent Sanguine. Those who knew her considered her a sweet, quiet, and gracious young lady. Six years ago she had the experience of being truly filled with the Holy Spirit. The change in her has been thrilling. I have watched a very fine person become a wonderful, exciting woman. The fears that had long enslaved her have largely been laid aside, causing a new release of pent-up sanguine impulses that formerly were squelched. I have watched my timid wife, who used to say, "I would be petrified if I had to speak to an audience," or "My husband is the speaker in our family," become a dynamic women's speaker who captivates an audience. Phlegmatics don't do that, but Sanguines do. As if witnessing a rosebud open into a beautiful flower, I have watched God take my reserved wife, who went four years without being asked to address small women's groups in our own church, take speaking engagements all over the West Coast. The last time I met her at the airport coming back from another state, I remarked, "If this keeps up I will soon be known as the husband of Beverly LaHaye."

Speaking is only one area of change in this former Phlegmatic-Sanguine. Old friends who see her today can hardly believe the outgoing, dynamic person she has become. If I were to diagnose her temperament at this stage of her life, I would be inclined to say she was more a Sanguine than a Phlegmatic — perhaps 55 percent Sanguine and 45 percent Phlegmatic. Naturally, much of the change in her reflects the modification of the Holy Spirit, but part of it is due to the elimination of childhood attitudes and habits that inhibited her sanguine temperament. The reason I know this change has been accomplished by the Holy Spirit is that her sanguine modifications have all been in the direction of strength. To my knowledge she has developed none of the characteristic weaknesses of the Sanguine.

This life points up the importance of childhood training. Next to leading your child to Christ, the greatest thing you can give him is an environment of love and understanding where he is at liberty to be himself. That does not mean indulgence, nor does it preclude discipline, but it does require that parents not force upon their children their own temperament hangups, but exercise patience, love, understanding, and self-control as it comes from the Holy Spirit. Every child must be treated as an individual. Some children must be disciplined severely in love, whereas others may be brought into line with only a disapproving look. But parents in particular need to be Spirit-controlled, that their prize possessions may grow up to fulfill all the potential of their individual abilities.

Another factor that can affect a person's behavior and create an erroneous impression of his natural temperament is trauma, either from a single experience or a series of events. These are more predominant in the fear areas, causing the individual to withdraw or recoil. For instance, some people who would ordinarily speak in public have had a traumatic experience that keeps them from trying. If a child attempts a part in the school play and is ridiculed instead of commended, he may develop a lifelong inhibition. Some people, when ill at ease, react nervously through inappropriate laughter or some other form of irregular behavior.

One Sanguine on the verge of a nervous breakdown at eight years of age was completely warped in personality. Instead of being a carefree, happy-go-lucky little chap, he was sullen most of the time. Anyone examining him in that condition would have concluded immediately that he was a very melancholy child. In reality, he had little or no melancholy temperament. The problem was his traumatic home life. His parents were divorced, but before their separation he was a constant witness to their endless feuds. This broke his sense of security, and when they took out their frustrations on him by screaming every time he made a noise or did something that displeased them, he built a protective shell around himself and nursed his grudges. I saw very little hope for the boy when the mother and the new stepfather brought him in. But after the parents received Christ, and as they grew in grace and knowledge of him, they showered the boy with the love and patience he desperately needed. The transformation is a testimony to the power of God. Today he is a senior in high school, and you would never suspect that this fun-loving young man was once a withdrawn eight-year-old. Obviously the love of Christ flowing through parents to children makes a difference in the way they develop.

One harmful misconception of temperament is that one type is better than another or that one combination is preferable to another. Kant thought the choleric was the best. Preacher Alexander Whyte preferred the sanguine-phlegmatic because it was outgoing and congenial, yet controlled. But God has made us all for "his good pleasure." No matter who we are, we possess strengths and weaknesses. The greater the weakness traits, the greater the strength traits. That is why highly gifted people often have so many emotional problems. If you are a person of great strengths, you will have great weaknesses. If you have average strengths, you will have average weaknesses. In addition, because "the pasture is always greener on the other side," people tend to want to be something they are not. I have seldom talked to a person who admitted, "I'm glad I am of the temperament I am," for we are all aware of our shortcomings and weaknesses. Unfortunately, we frequently magnify them and do not appreciate our strengths. This together with the power of habit can make anyone feel that his is the least desirable temperament of all.

Actually, the nature of one's temperament is incidental. If you have received Jesus Christ as your Lord and Savior, you have his Holy Spirit within you. He can so modify your weaknesses that the positive man or woman God wants you to be will dominate. Spirit-filled Christians are walking examples of transformed temperaments.

In the revelation of God's will for man found in the Bible, we read the accounts of many spiritual leaders. Several of these characters are classic examples of God's power to transform human temperament. We shall examine four such men in the remaining chapters. Please bear in mind that the modifying work of God in each of these men is available to you.

Repeatedly God said to Bible characters, "I am the God of Abraham, Isaac and Jacob . . ." meaning that his power was constant from one generation to another. In the New Testament we read that the Lord Jesus ". . . is the same yesterday, today, and forever." Since the power that transformed men in both the Old and New Testaments is available to us today, we can profit by seeing how God changed them.

4

PETER THE SANGUINE

Sanguine Peter is probably the best-loved character in the New Testament. The reason is quite simple. Because he is a complete extrovert, his shortcomings are open for everyone to see. As Peter impetuously stumbles through the pages of the Gospels, we see raw sanguine flesh. He is lovable and laughable one minute, downright disgusting the next. Peter is without question the most sanguine character in the Bible. Before proceeding farther we should examine the qualities of the sanguine temperament.

Mr. Sanguine is a warm, friendly, outgoing person who draws people like a magnet. He is a good talker, a happy-go-lucky optimist, "the life of the party." He is generous and compassionate, responsive to his surroundings and the moods or feelings of others. However, like the other three temperaments he has some natural weaknesses. He is often weak-willed, emotionally unstable and explosive, restless and egotistical. Voted "most likely to succeed" in his youth, he rarely measures up to expectations. He has great difficulty following through on details and is almost never quiet. Beneath his bold exterior he is often insecure and fearful. Sanguines make good salesmen, speakers, actors and, less frequently, leaders.

The Apostle Peter is the most prominent man in the four Gospels, aside from Jesus Christ, and is given considerable space in the first ten chapters of the book of Acts. He spoke more frequently than the other disciples and the Lord conversed more regularly with him. No disciple is given more severe reproof by our Lord, except Judas Iscariot, and, as far as we know, no other disciple had the effrontery to rebuke the Lord. On the other hand, no other disciple gave such outspoken testimony of his respect and love for Christ, and no other received such personal praise from the Savior.

Peter has a "charisma" about him that draws one to him, whether a first-century contemporary or a twentieth-century reader. That sanguine quality is probably what made Hippocrates determine that the temperament was caused by "warm blood." Certainly Peter exhibited warmth, intensity, and dynamic action. Alexander Whyte said of him, "The worst disease of the human heart is cold. Well, with all his faults, and he was full of them, a cold heart was not one of them. All Peter's faults, indeed, lay in the heat of his heart. He was too hot-hearted, too impulsive, too enthusiastic. His hot heart was always in his mouth, and he spoke it all out many a time when he should have held his peace." Peter was one of those transparent people who never kept his friends in doubt about his thoughts — he just blurted them out! This intense extrovertish tendency makes him the easiest temperament in the Bible to pick out.

The only person who finds it difficult to diagnose a sanguine temperament is Mr. Sanguine himself. He rarely scrutinizes his thoughts or actions but simply erupts as he bounds from one crisis to another. Many a Sanguine has sparked peals of laughter from his friends by declaring, "I just can't figure out which temperament I am." He is invariably the only one in doubt. Evidently he has very little analytical ability and is not given to self-examination or introspection.

Peter leaves the impression of a man of great physical stature as he strides through the first five books of the New Testament. We have no way of knowing, of course, since no description of him is given. Swashbuckling Sanguines who "make history rather than write it" usually are big men, and Peter was a swashbuckler! No matter what he did in life, Peter became the leader — he was born that way.

The completeness of the biblical record on Sanguine Peter makes him an excellent subject for this study. It is easy to diagnose his strengths and weaknesses, and the book of Acts offers enough details to demonstrate how the Holy Spirit strengthened his weaknesses. Instead of experiencing the usual frustrating futility of most Sanguines, Peter was so strengthened when filled with the Spirit that he stands as one of the most successful Sanguines we know. Not only was he the most influential man in the early church, but he continues to be a challenge to Christians as an example of what the Holy Spirit can do in the life of any man who will surrender to him.

Impulsive

When Andrew first brought his sanguine brother Simon to Jesus, he seemed anything but a promising spiritual leader. To the contrary, he was a boisterous, profane, opinionated fisherman whose most notable trait was impulsiveness. Whenever Peter acted, he acted instantaneously, now — or "straightway," as the Scripture states it. Whenever the conversational ball stopped bouncing, Peter picked it up. That is how he got his foot in his mouth so many times. He has often been called "the spokesman of the disciples." In fact, the words "then saith Peter" introduce more speeches than are recorded by all the other disciples together.

When Jesus called Peter, as described in Matthew 4:20, his impulsive response was to "straightway drop his nets and follow him." When Jesus' travels brought the disciples near Peter's home, he impulsively invited them all over to his house, not taking into consideration the fact that his mother-in-law was sick in bed (Mark 1:29). However, as so often occurs in the life of a Christian Sanguine, the Lord intervened, and this time he miraculously healed the woman, who then helped Peter's wife with the serving.

The impetuous sanguine temperament of Peter is clearly seen the night the Lord Jesus came to the disciples walking on the water. "And Peter . . . said, Lord, if it be thou, bid me come unto thee on the water. And . . . he walked on the water, to go to Jesus" (Matthew 14:28, 29). Who but an impulsive, boyish Sanguine would want to leave the safety of the boat to walk on top of the water?

This story also illustrates a common but less apparent trait of the Sanguine. In spite of his loud bravado, the Sanguine is generally quite fearful. He leaps before he looks and then becomes apprehensive about the consequences. That is exactly what happened to Peter. Having taken only a few steps on the water, instead of looking at the Lord, "when he saw the wind boisterous, he was afraid; and beginning to sink, he cried, saying, Lord, save me. And immediately Jesus stretched forth his hand, and caught him, and said unto him, O thou of little faith, why didst thou doubt?"

This common tendency of the Sanguine to leap before looking and then tremble at the possible consequences will be changed when the Holy Spirit fills his life. He will become "peaceful" and "self-controlled." He will "wait on the Lord" instead of running off half-cocked in every direction. Instead of becoming fearful, he will keep his eyes on the Lord rather than on his circumstances. Anyone who looks at circumstances will have doubts, but Peter is a good example of what to do when doubt, fear, or anxiety overtake you. He cried, "Lord save me," and Christ did.

Lest we are too unkind to Peter over his unbelief in this event, I would call your attention to the fact that he had enough faith at least to climb out of the boat onto the boisterous sea. That is more than can be said for the other disciples, some of whom could have profited from a little of his venturesome spirit.

One of Peter's outbursts offers us a humorous glimpse of his compulsion to talk. As one of the three favored disciples, Peter, together with James and John, was invited by the Lord to go up the Mount of Transfiguration (Matthew 17:1-13). Jesus was "transfigured before them; and his face did shine like the sun. . . ." These three men were given the privilege of seeing our Lord's divine glory shine through his humanity.

Then Moses and Elijah, two of the most respected men in the history of Israel, appeared "talking with them." Moved beyond control, as the Bible tells us, "Then answered Peter, and said unto Jesus, Lord, it is good for us to be here; if thou wilt, let us make here three tents; one for you, and one for Moses, and one for Elijah."

Whenever Mr. Sanguine doesn't know what to do, he talks. You can depend on him to break any period of strained silence with words — often ill-timed, unnecessary, or wrong. Such was the case with Peter. No one had asked him a question, yet he "answered" them. If ever there was a time for a man to keep his big mouth shut, this was it. But that didn't hinder Sanguine Peter. He had to say something, so he blurted out, "Lord, it is good for us to be here!" Isn't that classic? Here he is, treated to the rare privilege of seeing two men who died a thousand years earlier, and Peter blurts out, "It is good to be here." But that isn't enough, for our compulsive talker proceeds to suggest that they build three tents. Apparently it did not occur to him that the spirits of dead men don't need tents, and staying on top of the mountain would defeat our Lord's purpose in coming. Oh, I know Peter meant well — Mr. Sanguine usually does — but that doesn't change the fact that his ill-considered, impulsive ideas are often misdirected. On this occasion, he was so mistaken that Almighty God himself sounded from heaven the words, "This is my beloved Son, in whom I am well pleased; hear ye him!" Peter should have been listening, not talking.

The best-known illustration of Peter's impulsiveness occurred in the Garden of Gethsemane. The Lord Jesus had just drunk the "cup" of the new covenant in his blood and was ready to offer himself as the sacrifice for the sins of the world. Then "a great multitude with swords and clubs, from the chief priests and elders of the people," came out to take him by force. John tells us (18:10) that "Simon Peter, having a sword, drew it, and smote the high priest's servant, and cut off his right ear." Peter, of course, was a fisherman, not a swordsman. He probably aimed at his victim's head, but either the man ducked or Peter was out of practice, for all he got was an ear. Matthew suggests the reason for Peter's action when the Lord Jesus asked, "Thinkest thou that I cannot now pray to my Father, and he shall presently give me more than twelve legions of angels?" (26:53). That was Peter's problem — he just didn't think! Sanguines are activists, not thinkers. When the pressure is on, they must *do* something.

This lack of reflective thinking cheats many a Sanguine out of rich blessings in life. For instance, when Peter and the other disciples were brooding over the death of our Lord, some women came to report that they had been to the sepulcher, found it empty, and encountered an angel there who said, "He is not here; for he is risen, as he said" (Matthew 28:6). In characteristic manner, Peter rushed off to the tomb. John outran him, being a younger man, but he paused at the entrance of the empty tomb. When Peter arrived, he pushed past John and hurried into the tomb. Unlike John, who saw the evidence and believed that Christ had risen (John 20:8), Peter's emotions veiled the significance of the evidence that made a believer of John, and he went away sorrowful and confused. Only after the Lord appeared to him personally was Peter convinced that he had risen from the dead.

Another charming story which reveals Peter's impulsiveness occurred on the Sea of Galilee, after the resurrection of Christ. John tells us (21:1-11) of Peter's decision, "I go a fishing." As on a previous occasion, they "fished all night and caught nothing." Then Jesus appeared on the shore and called out to "cast the net on the right side of the boat, and ye shall find." They did, and suddenly they caught so many fish in their net that they were unable to pull it into the boat. John exclaimed, "It is the Lord!" When Peter heard that, he forgot all about the fish, cinched his cloak around him, and dived into the water to swim to Jesus. A typical Sanguine, he left the job unfinished when something more attractive appeared. We commend Peter for his love for Christ on this occasion, but he left the work to others, though he did lend them a hand when they came closer to shore. Sanguines are not lazy, but they tend to jump from one thing to another; they have a short interest span in one subject.

Uninhibited

Not all of Peter's impetuous actions were negative in effect. On several occasions he did or said the unexpectedly wonderful thing that warms your heart as you read the story. Sanguines have that pleasant capacity. Just about the time you are annoyed at their thoughtlessness, they do something that inspires your affection, and Peter was like that. It is very difficult not to love a Sanguine — often in spite of himself.

One such episode took place in the early days of our Lord's ministry (Luke 5:1-11). The people gathered close to him as he taught by the Sea of Galilee, so he stepped into Simon's boat and asked him to push it a little off shore. When he finished his message, Jesus turned to Peter and said, "Launch out into the deep, and let down your nets for a draught." Sanguine Simon, in a state of discouragement, replied, "Master, we have toiled all night, and have taken nothing." But right here one of his sanguine traits stood him in good stead, for Sanguines love to please. They delight in accommodating people and will often do anything rather than displease someone. Consequently he added, "Nevertheless, at thy word I will let down the net." No sooner had he let down his net than "they enclosed a great multitude of fishes; and their net broke . . . so that the boat began to sink."

Then it was that Sanguine Simon impulsively did something that endears him to the Christian's heart. Unashamedly and emotionally, in front of all his friends, he ". . . fell down at Jesus' knees, saying, Depart from me; for I am a sinful man, O Lord." This uninhibited bit of exhibitionism is typical of the Sanguine. Most people think Mr. Sanguine is a hypocrite or perhaps insincere because of his forthright public actions. That isn't true. He is a very uninhibited person and therefore tends impulsively to do whatever comes into his mind. It probably bothers him later, but at the moment he sincerely exhibits his internal self. Doubtless, such was the case with

Simon as he forgot all others and openly worshiped the Lord. Evidence of his sincerity is found in the fact that only a short time later he heeded the Master's call to leave his nets and follow him.

Outspoken

Another positive effect of Peter's impulsive tongue is found in Matthew 16:13-20. About midway in our Lord's three and one-half-year ministry he asked his disciples who men thought he was. They responded, "Some say thou art John the Baptist; some, Elijah; and others, Jeremiah, or one of the prophets." Then Jesus asked, "But whom say ye that I am?" Simon Peter instantly responded, "Thou art the Christ, the Son of the living God." This beautiful testimony so delighted the Savior that he replied, "Blessed art thou, Simon . . . flesh and blood has not revealed it unto you, but my Father, who is in heaven." Peter's testimony to Jesus' identity was the clearest given to that point in the Lord's life. It demonstrates that even then God was speaking to Peter's heart. Because Sanguines have a great capacity to respond enthusiastically to heart motivation, their hearts will compel them to walk in God's ways, if they will let God speak to them regularly from his Word. However, since the mind as well as experiences cause the heart to feel, it is very important to check the thoughts a Sanguine permits in his mind. I doubt that Peter premeditated his answer. He was not an analyzer, but he had heard Christ's matchless teachings and had seen his uniquely holy life for almost two years. He felt in his heart that this man was more than human — he was divine. So when asked the question, Peter simply stated how he felt. We are all indebted to Sanguine Simon for his inspiring answer.

Of all the events in the life of the sanguine apostle, my favorite is found in John 6:66-69. If this were the only event given of Peter's life, I think I could love him for this alone. The Lord Jesus was divine when he walked this earth, but he was also genuinely human. He was human enough to "hunger," to be "tired," to become "sorrowful," to "weep," and to be "moved with compassion." Such a time John relates to us toward the end of his ministry.

Many wanted to follow Jesus to receive the "loaves and fishes" and his healings, whereas Jesus wanted people to worship him for who he was and the truth he gave. So he started to emphasize the difficulties his followers would encounter if they decided to truly accept and follow him. This was too hard for many of them, for we read, "From that time many of his disciples went back, and walked no more with him." In what must have been a deep note of sadness, the Master turned to the twelve and inquired, "Will you also go away?" It was lovable, impulsive Peter who broke the silence with the immortal words, "Lord, to whom shall we go? Thou hast the words of eternal life! And we believe and are sure that thou art that Christ, the Son of the living God." In almost two thousand years, no man has eclipsed that classic statement.

Yes, Peter was all heart. But whenever that heart was fixed on Jesus Christ, he was 100 percent right. On the other hand, whenever his heart was fixed on others or himself, he was wrong. That problem is not limited to Sanguines! The success of any Christian's life is determined by the direction of his heart. That is why the Holy Spirit instructs us: "Set your affections on things above, not on things on the earth."

Egotistical

Another tendency of a sanguine person is egotism. Typical of the Sanguine, Peter couldn't stand success without letting it go to his head. In the very same chapter that Matthew told of Peter's excellent confession (Matthew 16), we see his tragic downfall. The Lord praised him in verse 17 for what he said and promised to give him "the keys to the kingdom of heaven." Later Peter, when filled with the Holy Spirit, used these keys in preaching the gospel to the Jews (Acts 2) and in first preaching the gospel to the Gentiles (Acts 10). But the fervent Sanguine had the gall to rebuke his Lord.

After Peter's confession, the Lord Jesus apparently began to prepare his disciples for the real purpose of his coming. He informed them that he "must go unto Jerusalem, and suffer many things from the elders and chief priests and scribes, and be killed, and be raised again the third day." Up to this point, Peter had accepted everything the Lord Jesus said, but the prospect of his death shocked Peter. He rejected the possibility so vehemently that he didn't seem to hear the Savior promise to ". . . rise again the third day." Sanguine Simon got so excited that he actually laid hands on Jesus, for it says, "Peter took him, and began to rebuke him. . . ." Whereas a few moments before he had acknowledged Jesus as the "Son of the living God," now he tried to correct him. The egotistical Sanguine proceeded to tell "the Christ, the Son of the living God" what to do. He exclaimed, "Be it far from thee, Lord; this shall not be unto thee" (Matthew 16:22). Sanguine Simon was wrong, for it did happen to him — Jesus was crucified. In fact, if it hadn't happened, we could never receive the forgiveness of sins.

Peter's impulsive action, motivated by egotism, earned him the most severe rebuke our Lord gave anyone except Judas Iscariot and the Pharisees. Turning to his sanguine disciple, the Lord charged, "Get thee behind me, Satan. Thou art an offense unto me; for thou savorest not the things that are of God, but those that are of men." Peter's spirit must have been crushed by the rebuke. The Bible doesn't tell us, but he probably moped for a while; Sanguines usually do. They tend to be easily offended, though they recover before long.

This story provides us with an excellent illustration of a common problem of the Sanguine. Peter's tendency toward egotism made him vulnerable to the devil's darts of pride. The Lord revealed that Satan gave Peter those words. Years later Peter offered some instruction in his first epistle (5:5-9) that may hark back to this event. He pictures the devil as "a roaring lion" who "walketh about, seeking whom he may devour."

When we read that text we may think of the devil trying to get Christians to deny the Lord, commit adultery, or perform some other gross form of sin. But Peter was writing about humility: "Humble yourselves, therefore, under the mighty hand of God . . ." Peter realized through his experience that the devil roars around seeking to fan egotistical inclinations into pride. But "pride bringeth a snare." Peter's fall was caused by letting the devil take the Lord's words of praise and fan them into a raging fire of pride. When we harbor pride, we quench the Holy Spirit's inward working, and soon pride is expressed in action that dishonors Christ. Egotistical Simon should stand as a warning to us that we resist this tendency to be proud, for in doing so we also resist the devil. Incidentally, Sanguines do not have a monopoly on this weakness.

Self-seeking

By nature Mr. Sanguine is very generous. If he sees someone in need, his emotional response is usually one of compassion. During the great depression, my sanguine father, with a wife and three children at home, was so moved by a cold, hungry boy that he impulsively gave him the last quarter he had in his pocket. That was commendable generosity motivated by the heart, not the mind. No doubt Peter was like that. But there is also tendency for Mr. Sanguine to feel insecure. This anxiety, together with a desire for prominence, probably caused Peter to make a self-seeking request.

The Lord Jesus used the "rich young ruler" as an example to teach his disciples how difficult it is for people who love their possessions to enter the kingdom of heaven. The sanguine disciple then asked, "Behold, we have forsaken all, and followed thee. What shall we have, therefore?" (Matthew 19: 27). This selfish thought was probably not unique to Peter, but it took a Sanguine to verbalize it. The Lord's reply reveals the nature of the true weakness when he said, "Many that are first shall be last, and the last shall be first." What was Peter's real problem? He was a first-century status seeker. There must be a little Sanguine in every man, because who can say he has never asked that very human question, "What am I going to get out of this?" Only the Holy Spirit can give us that consistent spirit of self-sacrifice so essential to an effective Christian.

Braggart

One of Mr. Sanguine's most apparent faults is his tendency to brag. Whatever he does or has is "the best." Even when he is successful, his temptation to brag or exaggerate makes his accomplishments disappointing. Give him enough rope and he will verbally hang himself. Such was the case that memorable night in the upper room when the Lord Jesus warned his disciples, "All ye shall be offended because of me this night; for it is written, I will smite the shepherd, and the sheep of the flock shall be scattered abroad" (Matthew 26:31). Blustering Peter couldn't let that prediction go unchallenged. Once again he contradicted the Lord by loudly proclaiming, "Though all men shall be offended because of thee, yet will I never be offended." The Lord then proceeded to tell Peter very pointedly that "before the cock crows, thou shalt deny me thrice." The sanguine one offered a very characteristic and vehement response: "Though I should die with thee, yet will I not deny thee." Doesn't that sound impressive? But the highway to success is not laid on a foundation of good intentions.

Peter's response on this occasion was sincere. One of the most misunderstood traits of a sanguine person is his sincerity. Have you ever noticed how quick and loud Mr. Sanguine is at making promises or commitments? When he doesn't follow through, or fails to pay, or arrives late, he gets the reputation of being insincere. Actually, he was very sincere when he made the promise — sincerely a Sanguine, that is. At the moment, in the upper room, being faithful to Jesus was all-important to Peter because he was in the Lord's presence. But Sanguines are very responsive to their environment. Away from the Lord, Mr. Sanguine was not able to keep his promise.

Weak-willed

Doubtless Mr. Sanguine usually means well. But one of his most serious difficulties is his weakness of will. Many a Sanguine is considered "a weak character" or "all mouth" by his contemporaries because he folds when the pressure is on. That weakness of will is probably what keeps him from reacting well under pressure.

Many a Sanguine will spontaneously lie under pressure rather than face shame or penalty. He will be sorry immediately, but unless strengthened by the Holy Spirit he will not have enough self-control to keep from doing the same thing again. Unaided by the power of God, Mr. Sanguine usually ensnares his carefree life with a tangled web of complexities.

Often in the counseling room, a very upset Mr. or Mrs. Sanguine has confessed a tragic series of events. Married to a loyal and faithful companion (opposites tend to attract each other), the Sanguine has committed the scarlet sin of adultery. It is an old story that comes through their tears. "I meant to keep my wedding vows!" is the piteous cry, and doubtless he did. But Mr. Sanguine's weakness of will makes it easy to forget past affirmations and intentions under the pressure of present temptation. One Sanguine businessman told me, "I love my wife and kids, but they were at home and that beautiful secretary was with me all day!" One thing I have noticed about sexual sins — they are invariably followed by lies and all kinds of deception. One lie leads to another, and it isn't long before Mr. Sanguine's short memory causes him to contradict himself. As the Bible says, "Be sure your sins will find you out."

Interestingly, Mr. Sanguine is usually relieved when he finally gets caught. The reason is quite simple: he can't stand pressure. The tangled web woven by unfaithfulness in marriage creates more guilt-pressure than the Sanguine can take. Being an emotional person, his repentance is accompanied by profuse weeping. Like Peter, Mr. Sanguine repents sincerely, and when he is filled with the Holy Spirit, tragedy can result in a life-changing experience; however, it is very important for him to realize that it isn't his strong resolutions or good intentions that produce consistency in his life. It is the Holy Spirit! Without the Holy Spirit, Mr. Sanguine cannot be trusted; but worse than that, he cannot trust himself.

Simon's denial

It is tragically true that the good things people do are not as well known as the bad. The one event best known in the life of our Lord's sanguine friend is his betrayal of the Savior. As Judas is known as "the disciple who betrayed him," Peter is known as "the disciple who denied him." All four Gospels tell us the shameful story. It may be that the Holy Spirit gave it four times to impress on us that God can take the most inconsistent and spineless lump of clay and fashion it into a mighty man of God.

A careful analysis of the events that surrounded Peter's denial supplies many interesting clues to the weakness of Mr. Sanguine. No one is more easily influenced by his environment than a Sanguine. That fact is not apparent when you first meet him. He comes on strong, almost overpowering sometimes, and gives the impression that he can master any situation. But that is not the case. Mr. Sanguine desperately needs the warmth of Christian fellowship.

In Peter's case, his troubles began when he left the disciples and joined the company of the enemy. "And the servants and officers stood there, who had made a fire of coals; for it was cold, and they warmed themselves; and Peter stood with them, and warmed himself" (John 18:18). It is always dangerous for a Christian to warm his hands at the enemy's fire, but particularly is that true of a Sanguine. He is sensitive to his associates and tends to adapt to their ways rather than stand alone in a crowd. Sanguines can act one way with one group of friends and quite another with a different group.

Matthew tells us that as Peter warmed his hands, a maid came by and said, "Thou also wast with Jesus of Galilee. But he denied it before them all, saying, I know not what thou sayest" (Matthew 26:69-70). The pressure of the group was too much for Sanguine Peter, and thus he denied the Lord whom he loved. He left the fire and walked out on the porch while Jesus was being tried inside. Then, "another maid saw him, and said unto them that were there, This fellow was also with Jesus of Nazareth. And again he denied with an oath, I do not know the man."

Many Sanguines since Peter have entertained the idea that if they could get off the hook just this once, then they would submit to God. Unfortunately, compromise never meets the standard. A small compromise may initiate a big compromise. Sooner or later we have to resist the pressure around us and take a stand. Happy is the man who learns that the sooner he faces the issue, the better off he is. Peter's instinctive desire to escape danger provoked him not only to repudiate allegiance to Christ, but to deny him "with an oath." He used a sign of honesty to cover his bald lie!

A short time later, others came to Peter. "Surely thou also art one of them; for thy speech betrayeth thee. Then began he to curse and swear, saying, I know not the man. And immediately the cock crowed." Peter's compulsion to talk kept him from being silent even while mingling with his enemies. Most of the people were city folk from Jerusalem, whereas Peter, from Galilee, had a different accent which "betrayed him."

An illustration of the progressive nature of sin is seen as the sanguine one, having denied his Lord twice, adds to the third denial the sin of cursing and swearing. Evidently, before his salvation Peter was a blasphemous character, often typical of the sanguine temperament. Most Sanguines tend to speak faster than they think, and in order to fill in the blank spaces they accumulate pet expressions that are often profane. Doubtless Peter did not use such language in the presence of the Lord, and possibly he had not used it for some time. But under group pressure and in a typical craving to be accepted by the people around him, Peter reached into his past and unconsciously resorted to his old language habit. When such a thing happens, a Sanguine is quick to explain, "Oh, I don't mean anything by it," but that does not change the fact that he has sinned with his tongue and publicly dishonored God.

Sanguine Simon, characteristically motivated by external stimuli, suddenly "remembered the word of Jesus" when he heard the cock crow. His reaction, recorded by all four of the Gospel writers, is typically sanguine: "And he went out, and wept bitterly." Only two temperaments in men are given to weeping: the sanguine and the melancholy. Contrary to popular notions, this does not lessen their manhood but reveals the depth of their feelings and the ability to express emotion.

Peter's bitter tears at the end of this tragic drama illustrate a typically sanguine trait. Sanguines are easy repenters. When Mr. Sanguine sins grievously, he is thoroughly remorseful when confronted with his sin or ensnared by the effects of it. Many modern Sanguines find their way to confession and sincerely weep in their expression of remorse. Observers sometimes think that depth of repentance is measured by the quantity of tears, whereas the tears only mean that Mr. Sanguine is sincere at that very moment. If he goes away to "warm his hands at the enemy's fire" again, it will be just a matter of time before he falls again.

The depth of Peter's remorse is evident in the tender scene recorded in the last chapter of the Gospel of John. After Jesus' resurrection he came to Peter and asked, "Simon Peter, lovest thou me more than these?" Peter responded, "Yes, Lord, you know that I love you." An important play on the Greek words originally used by our Lord and his sanguine apostle is not apparent in the English translation. The Lord Jesus used the word *"agape,"* which is the highest form of love used in the New Testament. In fact, it is the word used in describing the love of God for man. Peter, evidently because of great remorse at his tragic denial, was reluctant to use that word. His word for love is more akin to our word "like." In fact, some translators have rendered his reply, "You know, Lord, that I am very fond of you."

The Lord Jesus asked him again, "Simon, lovest thou me? He saith unto him, "Yea, Lord, thou knowest I am fond of thee." This response is identical to the first. But the third time the Lord Jesus changed his word in the original to Peter's word and asked, "Peter, are you fond of me?" "Peter was grieved because he said unto him the third time, Lovest thou me? And he said unto him, Lord, thou knowest all things; thou knowest that I am very fond of thee." It seems that the wound of Peter's great denial was so fresh and so deep that the sanguine apostle had finally learned an invaluable lesson. Peter had discovered that he could not trust himself. The only hope for a Sanguine is in a life dependent on the Holy Spirit. Peter seemed to realize that he could not trust his emotions, therefore he was reluctant to give a glib answer and excessively commit himself. Instead, he wanted to prove his love by his actions. This life-changing decision seems to characterize most of Peter's life from this point on, evidence that even an inconsistent Sanguine can become a stable, usable instrument when filled with the Holy Spirit.

Simon's inconsistency

The previous story and many other events in the life of Peter indicate that one of Mr. Sanguine's greatest problems is inconsistency. His life seems to be a paradox of extremes. He is hot one minute and cold the next. That Mr. Sanguine himself is displeased with this tendency and disgusted with himself because of it I have no doubt. The Lord Jesus seemed to know that the longing of Simon's sanguine heart was to be a stable individual. For that reason, he prophetically changed his name, saying, "Thou art Peter . . ." meaning, thou art a stone. That Peter became strong when filled with the Holy Spirit is now history.

When a man receives Jesus Christ into his life he becomes a "new creature." Thus he has two natures, the old and the new. Peter's two names are typical of the two natures of every believer. "Simon" represents the old sanguine nature, whereas "Peter" represents the new rocklike nature, the stable consistent man molded by the Spirit of God out of the sanguine temple of clay. However, as illustrated in the life of Peter, this change is not immediate; it is a matter of growth.

John tells us in the second chapter of his first epistle, "I have written unto you, young men, because ye are strong . . .

and ye have overcome the wicked one." Baby Christians do not overcome the old nature. Only as we mature in Christ and are controlled by the Holy Spirit does the new man control the old. This change is more evident in the sanguine temperament than in any other. The reason for that is quite simple: everything the Sanguine does, whether good or bad, is conspicuous. The other, less volatile, temperaments are less noticeable in behavior. In fact, sometimes wrong conduct is not recognized as such, because it is not extreme. God, however, looks on the heart. The changing of Peter's name by the Master Changer of men is a good example of what he wants to do for every human being. The Spirit-controlled man will not cease to be "himself." We shall see that the change that eventually came into Peter's life did not eliminate his temperament, but modified it. After the filling of the Holy Spirit, Sanguine Simon no longer erupts in uncontrolled behavior. Instead, as Sanguine Peter he is controlled in his actions. The dynamic, lovable, magnetic characteristics of Sanguine Peter are still evident, as we shall see, but the weaknesses are modified by the strengths, and God is glorified in the transformation.

Peter's filling

As one of his promises to his disciples, our Lord said, "But ye shall receive power, after that the Holy Spirit is come upon you. . . ." We usually think of this power in the framework of witnessing, and certainly it means that. But that is not all it means. The power of the Holy Spirit in the life of the sanguine apostle was an obvious influence for good. That power, available to every believer today, so modified Peter that it obscured his weaknesses and revealed his strengths. As we study this Spirit-controlled Sanguine in the book of Acts, let us keep in mind that God is no respecter of persons. What he did for his sanguine apostle he will do for you — if you are willing to cooperate with the Holy Spirit and let his power strengthen your weaknesses.

The first sign of change in the Apostle Peter is seen in Acts 1:15, even before the Day of Pentecost. He "stood up in the

48

midst of the disciples" when they were gathered together for prayer while awaiting the coming of the Holy Spirit. This is Peter's first recorded sermon, apparently a funeral message for Judas Iscariot.

As we scrutinize the message we find no exaltation of Peter but, instead, a Spirit-filled message based on the Word of God, offering a practical solution to the vacancy of the traitor Judas. Peter then proposed a very practical standard for his replacement: ". . . Of these men who have companied with us all the time that the Lord Jesus went in and out among us, beginning from the baptism of John unto that same day that he was taken up from us; must one be ordained to be a witness with us of his resurrection." In other words, the twelfth apostle should have been with the other apostles all during Jesus' ministry. He then prayed and asked the Lord for wisdom. They selected two candidates and, as was their custom, relied on the Holy Spirit to choose the right one through the casting of lots. We no longer cast lots in such matters, for since the Day of Pentecost we have the indwelling Holy Spirit to guide us in making our decisions, but on that side of Pentecost, Peter's action was commendable and in keeping with Old Testament practice.

On the Day of Pentecost we get another thrilling insight into the transformation of the sanguine apostle. When the Holy Spirit came upon men, they spoke in the languages of foreign visitors to Jerusalem so that everyone heard God's message in his "own tongue." The Jerusalemites, who could not understand these languages, began to mock the disciples and jumped to the conclusion that "these men are full of new wine."

It was a Spirit-controlled Sanguine Peter who, "standing up with the eleven, lifted up his voice, and said unto them, Ye men of Judaea, and all ye that dwell at Jerusalem. . . ." and preached the first gospel sermon of the church age. His sermon is a masterpiece that cannot be explained by three years of association with Jesus Christ. Peter was an uneducated fisherman. He was not an intellectual; Sanguines rarely are. This sermon was the message of God through the instrument of

Sanguine Peter, a classic example of the way God wants to use men today. As you well know if you have studied the second chapter of Acts, the result was that "the same day there were added unto them about three thousand souls. And they continued steadfastly in the apostles' doctrine and fellowship." The stumbling, inconsistent, emotionally unstable Sanguine Simon was transformed into a Spirit-controlled Sanguine Peter, a mighty preacher of the gospel.

Sanguine men usually make good speakers, but only Spirit-controlled Sanguines make good preachers. Sanguine preachers have a built-in danger. It is easy for them to speak whether or not they have anything substantial to say, for a natural Sanguine has the ability of making anything sound interesting. But a Spirit-controlled Sanguine can be a mighty influence for God.

It is not too difficult to tell when Mr. Sanguine is speaking by Spirit or the "flesh." Speaking under the influence of his sanguine temperament, he will emphasize "I" and the message will remind hearers of Shakespeare's "Words, Desdemona, words!" Like Peter on the Day of Pentecost, Mr. Sanguine under the controlling influence of the Holy Spirit will glorify Jesus Christ. The Spirit-controlled sanguine pastor will overcome his great temptation of flitting here and there in restless activity and discipline himself for sufficient study of the Word of God to deliver a message from God rather than a charismatic, spontaneous sanguine speech. Spiritually astute listeners will notice the difference.

Peter's consistency

The third chapter of Acts assures us that Peter's power on the Day of Pentecost was not an emotional outburst or a fleeting trust in God. Instead, we find Peter and John going together "into the temple at the hour of prayer." Spiritual discipline is very difficult for Mr. Sanguine, but that is the only way his inconsistency will be eliminated. Melancholy John would naturally do the right thing in going up to the house of prayer at the designated hour. But a prayer meeting is only attractive to Mr. Sanguine when he is controlled by the Holy Spirit.

Another characteristic of the Spirit is seen in this story. When he controls our lives, we are not going to be "up tight" or fearful. A fruit of the Holy Spirit is "peace." This means in a practical sense that we will be flexible and "available" to whatever the Holy Spirit would have us do. Peter and John went to the temple to pray, relaxed in the Spirit, but when they saw the crippled man begging at the gate, they were moved with compassion and their plans changed entirely. As a matter of fact, they didn't get to the temple to pray. For Peter, "fastening his eyes upon him, with John, said, Look on us. . . . Silver and gold have I none, but, such as I have, give I thee. In the name of Jesus Christ of Nazareth, rise up and walk. And he took him by the right hand, and lifted him up; and immediately his feet and ankle bones received strength."

What is missing in this story? Close scrutiny will reveal the absence of Sanguine Simon. Spirit-controlled Peter in no way seeks to glorify himself but gives all glory to the Lord Jesus Christ in the healing of this man. This seems to be a hallmark for Sanguine Peter. Led by the Holy Spirit, Peter seizes the opportunity presented by the crowd that gathers to see the healed man leaping and shouting for joy, and he preaches a marvelous sermon, showing unusual depth and understanding. The Holy Spirit's participation is seen in the results: "Many of them who heard the word believed; and the number of the men was about five thousand" (Acts 4:4).

Peter's courage

The news that thousands of people who had clamored for the death of Jesus Christ a few weeks earlier were now repenting of that sin and openly confessing him as Lord and Savior did not set well with the Jewish officials. The chief priests summoned the apostles before them for interrogation. It was Spirit-controlled Sanguine Peter who answered their charges, giving all glory to Jesus Christ. The Scripture tells us that "when they saw the boldness of Peter and John, and perceived that they were unlearned and ignorant men, they marveled; and they took knowledge of them, that they had been with Jesus."

A short time before, cowardly Peter had denied his Lord three times. Now, under even greater pressure, he boldly acknowledged Jesus Christ. His remarks do not reveal sanguine bravado, but instead a fearless commitment to a condemned Man. What made the difference in Peter's reactions under pressure? Acts 4:8 explains it clearly: "Then Peter, filled with the Holy Spirit, said unto them. . . ." Peter did not strive to gain boldness under pressure; instead he relaxed and was impelled by the Holy Spirit. This should always be the case with a Christian facing a witnessing opportunity.

A college student asked me: "Why do I always get up tight and nervous when I go to witness to someone on campus?" I explained that this common experience occurs when we are relying on our own gifts and skill, though we may be sincerely concerned. The best way to witness to our faith comes through yielding ourselves to the Holy Spirit.

If you are on an elevator with a person who may need to hear about Christ, you are not responsible to force a conversation. You are responsible, however, to make your lips available to the Holy Spirit. I used to struggle with introductory clichés or "door openers," but with very little success. The most thrilling conversions that I have witnessed have resulted from a simple prayer in the presence of a sinner, "Lord, here are my lips; if you want to use them to share Christ with this person, I'm available." I would relax, and if I found myself conversing and we verged on spiritual things, as frequently happens, I was confident the Holy Spirit was making a witness. But if the conversation didn't move into spiritual matters, though I was willing, I was equally confident that I was led by the Holy Spirit. I don't always know the mind of the Holy Spirit and what he does in and through my life, nor am I responsible for what he does. I am responsible, as Sanguine Peter was, to be available, and so are you. This kind of witnessing is more effective because it permits control by the Holy

Spirit. If there must be pressure, put the "pressure" on the Holy Spirit by yielding yourself to him. He can stand pressure — you can't.

The most remarkable illustration from my own life of the Holy Spirit's using my available lips took place on a 707 jet between Chicago and San Diego. Dog-tired after a week of meetings, I boarded the plane, hoping to sleep all the way home. It was very crowded, and I happened to see a man who vaguely recognized me. He invited me to sit next to him and then suddenly turned pale, for he recalled that I was the minister who had prayed at a public meeting about a year before. If he had remembered that sooner, he never would have invited me to sit next to him.

This aeronautical engineer, who had been a squadron commander in the Air Force and was spared from death many times, was returning from a ten-day inspection tour. The last thing he wanted to do — I found out later — was talk to a minister, but he bravely and politely made the best of the situation. During the first of the four hours on that flight we got into an in-depth political conversation, one of my few secular hobbies. The conversation was so far removed from anything spiritual that I prayed, "Lord, I know you had me meet this man for a reason, but how in the world I will get the conversation around to spiritual things I cannot imagine. Here are my lips. I am available for whatever you have for us."

Within five minutes that man jumped a conversational ocean and said, "Say, you're a theologian; I wonder if you would answer a question for me. My brother-in-law has been talking to me about religion and I don't understand what he is trying to say. Would you explain to me what it means to be born again?" In more than twenty-five years of sharing Jesus Christ with individuals, I have never had a better opportunity, and it came exclusively through the power of the Holy Spirit. Long before we got to San Diego, this veteran flyer bowed his head and invited Jesus Christ into his life. The Holy Spirit isn't looking for clever people, but for available people.

Peter's wisdom

Most individuals do not think well under pressure. Usually our best ideas come long after an argument. But this was not the case with Sanguine Peter when controlled by the Holy Spirit. Under the pressure of interrogation by religious authorities, whom he had held in high esteem all his life, Peter's mind was clear as a bell. Then the authorities commanded Peter and John "not to speak at all nor teach in the name of Jesus." Peter and John did not vacillate and stammer before these brilliant leaders, nor did Peter emotionally utter things detrimental to his testimony. Instead, he said to them, "Whether it is right in the sight of God to hearken unto you more than unto God, judge ye. For we cannot but speak the things which we have seen and heard." This wisdom and emotional control is foreign not only to Sanguine Peter, but to any Sanguine. The disciples left their oppressors, celebrated by conducting a prayer meeting, and did not cease to speak "the word of God with boldness" (Acts 4:31).

Further evidence of the divine perception given to Sanguine Peter, the leader of the early Church, is seen in the unique way he handled the Ananias and Sapphira affair in Acts 5. There was no bitterness nor animosity in the way he dealt with them, but these two who had defrauded the Spirit before the people were exposed and slain as an example to the early Church. The whole thing was handled in a moderate manner that was foreign to Sanguine Simon but a common experience to Spirit-controlled Sanguine Peter.

Another example of Spirit-inspired wisdom occurred when Peter stood before the council and was rebuked by the high priest for trying to "bring this man's blood upon us." Peter did not become angry, as was his sanguine inclination, but instead, under the control of the Spirit, he wisely answered, "We ought to obey God rather than man."

Even when pressured by man to do wrong, the Spirit-controlled Christian does not have to get upset, resentful, or vitriolic. He can always do right without grieving the Holy Spirit. Sanguines must bear this in mind concerning flesh-motivated anger. Since "God's grace is sufficient for you" under all circumstances, you never have to "blow your top" or ruin your testimony by other hostile conduct. Your victory does not depend on someone else's behavior! Humanly speaking, you may have several reasons to get angry, but you have divine resources within you to respond in peace. The secret is in recognizing you are sunk the moment you indulge yourself by thinking: "He has no right to do that to me." Never respond in kind, but in the Spirit.

Even when Mr. Sanguine is controlled by the Holy Spirit, he is going to be enthusiastic and extrovertish. God made him that way. But sometimes his forceful response to situations is erroneously interpreted as hostility. He will have to be watchful of this, particularly around non-Christians because they expect Christians to be calm and serene.

Peter's joy

Joy is a natural tendency of the sanguine temperament. Ordinarily Mr. Sanguine not only takes pleasure in what he does but he has a way of making folks around him enjoy life. However, he does have a tendency to be easily offended, and his enjoyment may be turned into grousing or griping about the way people have treated him or the way things have turned out. This will produce a period of depression which is usually dissipated by the first external object that comes into view.

Peter's reaction to being severely beaten by the Sanhedrin officials is the reverse of what we would expect from a Sanguine. In Acts 5:41 we read, "And they departed from the presence of the council, rejoicing that they were counted worthy to suffer shame for his name." This reaction is evidence of Spirit-control. In Ephesians 5 we find that one of the first characteristics of the Spirit-filled life is a rejoicing heart. That is the reason Peter went on his way "rejoicing" instead of grumbling. Any Christian seeking to walk in the Spirit will examine his speech. When you find yourself griping, criticizing, grumbling, or using other verbal expressions of complaint, it is evidence that you are not controlled by the Spirit. The Holy Spirit will give us a spontaneous inclination to rejoice, thus fulfilling "the will of God in Christ Jesus concerning you" (1 Thessalonians 5:18).

Peter's humility

Humility is definitely not a characteristic of the Sanguine. Mr. Sanguine's natural egotistical traits cause him to be a glory seeker. For that reason he rarely does anything obscurely just to help people, but accomplishes everything with fanfare and staging to give him as much recognition as possible. This is certainly not the case with Spirit-controlled Sanguine Peter. An excellent illustration is found in Acts 9:36-42. Dorcas, a woman "full of good works and almsdeeds," became ill and died. As Peter was in Joppa, her home city, the leaders of the church sent for him. Peter's conduct, recorded in verses 39-42, is a classic example of how the Holy Spirit modifies a sanguine egotist.

"Then Peter arose and went with them. When he was come, they brought him into the upper chamber; and all the widows stood by him weeping, and showing the coats and garments which Dorcas made, while she was with them. But Peter put them all forth, and kneeled down, and prayed; and turning to the body said, Tabitha, arise. And she opened her eyes; and when she saw Peter, she sat up. And he gave her his hand, and lifted her up; and when he had called the saints and widows, presented her alive. And it was known throughout all Joppa; and many believed in the Lord."

What could bring more glory to one's reputation than raising the dead? Yet Peter insisted that they all leave the room so that no one could observe what he did. He enjoyed the privacy that gave the glory exclusively to God. Such conduct is so foreign to a man of Peter's native temperament that it has to be the work of the Holy Spirit.

Peter's prayerfulness

A perennial difficulty with most sanguine Christians is a lack of consistency in their devotional habits. Restless by nature, they find it easy to flit around, engaging in all kinds of "activities for the Lord," without spending much time with him personally in prayer and Bible study. In themselves many sanguine Christians are very shallow and prone to be carnal in their decisions, but time spent in daily Bible study and prayer seems to make a strong impact on them.

The tenth chapter of Acts reveals an exciting experience in the life of Spirit-controlled Sanguine Peter. Little did he know as he went on the housetop to pray that this would lead to his second use of the "keys of the kingdom" — the opening of heaven to the Gentiles through the gospel. As he prayed, he had a vision of a sheet lowered from heaven bearing all kinds of four-footed beasts, and he was instructed to "kill and eat." Verse 19 tells us, "While Peter thought on the vision, the Spirit said unto him . . ." Many a sanguine Christian lacks guidance by the Spirit because his restless activity keeps him from talking to and hearing from the Lord.

Peter's love

This same story reveals another modification of Sanguine Peter by the Holy Spirit. Sanguines are prone to be opinionated and biased. One rarely has to guess the degree of their bigotry, for they are prone to blurt it out. Frequently they welcome a chance to argue with such outbursts. Once having made up their minds, they tend to refuse evidence to the contrary, and thus it is difficult to get them to alter their opinions. Before Pentecost, Peter revealed these characteristics abundantly, but now, controlled by the Holy Spirit, things were different. As a good Israelite he had an ingrained antagonism toward all Gentiles, particularly Roman soldiers. Now the Spirit of God was instructing him to go to Cornelius, a Roman centurion, and tell him the gospel. Peter's response was one of immediate obedience (verse 21).

Cornelius, deeply convicted by the Holy Spirit, welcomed Peter "and fell down at his feet, and worshiped him. But Peter took him up, saying, Stand up; I myself also am a man." This humble reaction by Peter testified again to the controlling influence of the Holy Spirit.

Even before Peter knew the nature of his errand or the deep change God had wrought, he revealed his objective concern for the alien Gentiles. He said, "Ye know that it is an unlawful thing for a man that is a Jew to keep company, or come unto one of another nation; *but God* has shown me that I should not call any man common or unclean. Therefore came I unto you without objection, as soon as I was sent for" (verses 28, 29). This story illustrates that it was not just Peter's mouth that was sanctified, but his entire attitude and motivation. Peter was determined to be completely available to the living God. Verse 28 conveys the key to such temperament modification: *"but God."* These two words guarantee help for every undisciplined, opinionated, egotistical, weak-willed Sanguine. God the Holy Spirit proves a strength for every human weakness.

Because he was available to the Holy Spirit, Peter preached a Spirit-filled message that offered salvation to these Gentiles. The response was electrifying! "The Holy Spirit fell on all them who heard the word." Even though the Jews who accompanied Peter were astonished, he led the new converts into water baptism; "And he commanded them to be baptized in the name of the Lord."

Peter's gentleness

The characteristic sanguine tendency to be rough, impatient, and much like the proverbial "bull in the china shop" had left Peter. He was so Spirit controlled that we find nothing but grace and gentleness. When he returned to Jerusalem, "they that were of the circumcision (Jewish legalists) contended with him." Typical of flesh-controlled Christians, they couldn't see over their critical bias to the harvest of souls. Instead of lashing out at them, the normal reaction of Sanguine Simon, we find that Peter gently "reviewed the matter from the beginning, and expounded it in order unto them." And he gave them all the details.

Because of his Spirit-controlled and gentle explanation, they responded to this first harvest of Gentile outsiders, for the Scripture tells us, "When they heard these things, they held their peace, and glorified God, saying, Then hath God also to the Gentiles granted repentance unto life." Sanguine Simon knew nothing about the principle that grace and gentleness turn away angry criticism, but the Holy Spirit did. Instead of inciting a fight and division, Peter drew the people closer together. We cannot help but ask ourselves if many of the shameful conflicts of the past nineteen hundred years of church history would have been avoided had the leaders faced their critics under the controlling influence of the Holy Spirit. This challenge, of course, is not limited to those of sanguine temperament.

Peter's faith

One of the nine characteristics of the Spirit-filled life, according to Galatians 5:22, 23, is faith. As we have already seen, Mr. and Mrs. Sanguine have a tendency to be fearful. This is particularly true when they must face decisions alone. The twelfth chapter of Acts presents Sanguine Peter in a completely different light. Herod the King had imprisoned some of the leaders of the church because he wanted to "vex" them. Peter, alone and in jail, was sent for by Herod (12:6). Instead of fretting and fuming because of the confinement or worrying about his security, Peter was peacefully sleeping when the angel suddenly appeared to set him free. To sleep under such conditions could only mean that Peter was relaxed and fearless in the care of his heavenly Father.

Peter's patience

Sanguine people have a tendency to be sarcastic to the point of emotional injury of their friends. As a counselor I have come to believe that most people have sarcastic thoughts but tend to keep them to themselves. Not so Mr. Sanguine. He blurts out almost everything that comes into his head.

After Peter's miraculous delivery by the angel, he "came to the house of Mary, the mother of John . . . where many were gathered together praying. And as Peter knocked at the door of the gate, a maid came to hearken, named Rhoda. And when she knew Peter's voice, she opened not the gate for gladness, but ran in, and told how Peter stood before the gate. And they said unto her, Thou art mad. But she constantly affirmed that it was even so. Then said they, It is his angel." What was the naturally impatient Peter doing while the unbelieving prayer warriors were doubting the answer to their own prayers? Patiently, "Peter continued knocking."

Instead of greeting them with a blast of sarcasm, the Scripture tells us that Peter, "beckoning unto them with the hand to hold their peace, declared unto them how the Lord had brought him out of the prison." If ever there was an opportunity for a church leader to slash his friends, this was it. But Peter was more concerned about their spiritual encouragement and the grace of God than in ridiculing others' weakness. Chapter 12 is a vivid demonstration of the work of the Holy Spirit in a sanguine temperament.

Peter's leadership

The Spirit-inspired leadership of the sanguine apostle becomes apparent in the 15th chapter of Acts at a crucial moment in the early Church's history. Paul and Barnabas had just returned from their first missionary journey among the Gentiles. The reaction of legalistic Christians was bitter, creating "no small dissension and disputation with them." Paul and Barnabas appeared before the elders, declaring "all things that God had done with them. But there rose up certain of the sect of the Pharisees who believed, saying that it was needful to circumcise them and to command them to keep the law of Moses. . . . And when there had been much disputing, Peter rose up." The speech of Peter in the face of these hostile circumstances was used of the Holy Spirit to bring unity again to the early Church. For we read that when he had finished, "then all the multitude kept silence, and listened to Barnabas and Paul, declaring what miracles and wonders God had wrought among the Gentiles by them."

One of the things that keeps most Sanguines from being good leaders over a long period of time is their immaturity. It is difficult for them to be objective, and in the heat of battle they get so involved that instead of acting as oil on the water they become a source of irritation. This usually limits the effectiveness of their leadership. However, such natural tendencies are excluded from this record of Peter's behavior. The only explanation for Peter's acting in such an unusual manner is the control of the Holy Spirit.

Proof that Peter was an effective leader in the early days of the young Church is supplied for us by the Apostle Paul in Galatians 2:8. Paul was an intellectual with superb training, yet in these words he paid high tribute to the leadership ability of his sanguine friend, the Apostle Peter. "For he that wrought effectually in Peter to the apostleship of the circumcision . . ." offers a contemporary testimony to the miraculous results in Peter's Spirit-modified temperament.

Peter's lapse

It would be a mistake to think that after the Day of Pentecost Peter was always Spirit controlled. Idealistic Christians tend to set up standards so unreal that it is impossible to maintain them. Then in discouragement some stop trying to walk in the Spirit. As we shall see, the New Testament shows that Peter was not always controlled by the Holy Spirit after the Day of Pentecost.

Although God is interested in every experience of our lives and commands us to walk in holiness, he is not waiting to punish us for failure. King David is known in the Bible as "the man after God's own heart," not because he was perfect, but because he repented after sinning and turned contritely to God for forgiveness and restoration of grace. God did not cease blessing the king after his gross sins, but he sent conviction through Nathan the prophet and welcomed David back into fellowship. Even Elijah became so depressed that he asked God to let him die. God forgave the great prophet and used him mightily afterward. Because Christians cannot escape "flesh" impulses, Galatians 5:16 urges us: "Walk in the Spirit, and ye shall not fulfill the lust of the flesh." This challenge was not given to godless people but to Christians. Instead of becoming depressed over our sins and perpetuating carnality by self-abasement, erring Christians should immediately invoke the confession of 1 John 1:9 and enjoy God's complete forgiveness and forgetfulness of sin.

Peter's reversion to Sanguine Simon is recorded by the Apostle Paul in Galatians 2. It seems that when Peter was with Paul at Antioch, "he did eat with the Gentiles," because the church of Antioch contained a large number of Gentile converts. But when "certain men came from James . . . he withdrew and separated himself, fearing them who were of the circumcision." The Apostle Paul said that in doing so "they walked not uprightly according to the truth of the gospel" (Galatians 2:14). Somehow Sanguine Peter turned back to Sanguine Simon because of "fear." The fear of man is particularly characteristic of the Sanguine. Peter did not want to receive the displeasure of his friends, so he separated himself from his Gentile brethren and no doubt offended them. This certainly did not indicate that God ceased to use Peter's life, for his two epistles were written long after this event. It does, however, suggest that even mature, Spirit-filled Christians must "take heed to themselves" lest they, too, walk in the flesh momentarily.

Peter's maturity

The apostle's spiritual maturity is seen in a number of events that took place after this. But perhaps the outstanding occasion was his meekness after the Apostle Paul had "withstood him to the face" (Galatians 2:11). Instead of resenting Paul's rebuke, Peter demonstrated loving appreciation. In his second epistle, written near the end of his life, we find this whole-hearted tribute to the Apostle Paul as it came from the pen of Sanguine Peter: "The longsuffering of our Lord is salvation, even as our beloved brother, Paul, also according to the wisdom given unto him, hath written unto you" (2 Peter 3:15). Peter further commends the epistles of Paul, and in verse 16 puts them on a par with the Old Testament Scriptures. This is probably the greatest tribute one Jewish Christian could pay to another — acknowledging the work of God in Paul's life as in the life of Moses, David, Daniel, and Samuel.

The transformation of the sanguine apostle graphically demonstrates that God is able to make *you* the kind of person he wants you to be. It also shows that for every inherited weakness, even those increased in intensity through habit, there is a cure. God the Holy Spirit has a strength for every one of the weaknesses of the Sanguine. Mr. Sanguine, like every other Christian, continually needs to heed the admonition: "Be filled with the Spirit" (Ephesians 5:18).

5

PAUL THE CHOLERIC

The best illustration of choleric temperament among Bible characters is found in the Apostle Paul. He is also the best illustration of transformed choleric temperament. In fact, he is an excellent example of the way the Holy Spirit modifies a strong-willed person after conversion. Very few of Saul's pre-Christian activities are revealed in Scripture, and over 95 percent of his recorded experiences took place after he was filled with the Holy Spirit. Nevertheless, he walks through the pages of the book of Acts with a heavy choleric foot. A modified Choleric, yes, a Spirit-controlled Choleric, yes, but every inch a Choleric. Before we make a detailed study of this choleric apostle, let's examine the characteristics of a choleric person.

Mr. Choleric is a practical activist. All of life is utilitarian to him. He is strong willed, a natural leader, and very optimistic. His brain is filled with ideas, projects, or objectives, and he usually sees them through. Like Mr. Sanguine, he is extrovertish, but not nearly as intense. Although very productive in life, he has serious natural weaknesses. He is self-sufficient, impetuous, hot-tempered, and has a tendency to be harsh or cruel. No one can be as cutting and sarcastic as a Choleric. They make good supervisors, generals, builders, crusaders, politicians, or organizers, but are not usually able to do precise detail work.

Saul of Tarsus was not only raw choleric temperament, but a well-educated and very religious Choleric. So it should not surprise us that the first time Saul of Tarsus comes on the scriptural scene he is participating in the stoning of Stephen, the first recorded Christian martyr.

After a magnificent sermon by Stephen, the Spirit-filled "deacon," the antagonistic religious leaders lashed out against him. "When they heard these things, they were cut to the heart, and they gnashed on him with their teeth" (Acts 7:54).

When Stephen revealed his vision of heaven and the Lord Jesus standing at the right hand of the throne of God, the Scripture tells us that "they cried out with a loud voice, and stopped their ears, and ran upon him with one accord, and cast him out of the city, and stoned him; and the witnesses laid down their clothes at a young man's feet, whose name was Saul." Some have suggested that placing their clothes at Saul's feet indicated his leadership of the group. Some scholars further suggest that Choleric Saul was a member of the Sanhedrin, the select council of seventy elders in Israel. It was an esteemed honor to be on this council, and for a young man it was particularly unusual. Such suggestion is taken from Acts 26:10, where the choleric apostle acknowledges that in his younger years he had testified against the Christians in Jerusalem before the chief priests. Saul voted there that they "be put to death." In any case, Acts 8:1 shows that "Saul was consenting unto his death" — referring to Stephen.

Cruel

From this hostile beginning Saul continued his harsh, cruel way so characteristic of the choleric temperament. Most of the world's cruel dictators and criminals have been predominantly of the choleric temperament. One of the hardest things for a Christian Choleric to learn is to exhibit the "milk of human kindness." He is often blunt, verbally sarcastic, and cutting with his tongue.

Two couples at a fair decided to have their handwriting analyzed by an IBM computer, and the Choleric in the group was the first to volunteer. His wife and friends of over twenty years erupted in peals of laughter when they saw his card which read: "You have a strong tendency to be blunt and sarcastic." Their spontaneous laughter verified that the computer was right on target. Ordinarily it is easy to tell when a Choleric is Spirit-filled, because his speech will be flavored with Spirit-motivated kindness and grace instead of cutting, biting, or nasty remarks. This is true also of his deeds.

Choleric Saul tramples his cruel way through the early chapters of the book of Acts, leading the "great persecution against the Church which was at Jerusalem." Seemingly his hatred for Christians and his ruthless attempt to destroy them was inspired by religion. History reveals that many a Choleric has perpetrated inhuman deeds in the name of religion. Some have even used Christianity as a cloak to hallow their wrath and justify their hateful deeds.

The Scripture describes Choleric Saul as "breathing out threatenings and slaughter against the disciples of the Lord." Like most Cholerics who have a tendency to be cunning and crafty when motivated by hatred and ruthlessness, Saul "went unto the high priest, and desired of him letters to Damascus to the synagogues, that if he found any of this way [Christians in the early days of the Church] whether they were men or women, he might bring them bound unto Jerusalem" (Acts 9: 1-2). With these documents of authority in his hands, Saul was a fire-breathing vigilant with the power of life or death for enemies of the people. One of the men who lived in Damascus at this time, Ananias, acknowledged that he knew how "much evil (harm) he had done." In fact, because of Saul's former brutality, Ananias hesitated to believe the Holy Spirit's message that this powerful enemy had been converted.

This is almost the extent of our knowledge of Saul's pre-Christian activities, but it is sufficient to establish his native temperament as choleric. No doubt he had a secondary temperament, as do all people. It is sometimes difficult to determine the secondary temperament, as we mentioned in chapter 3, but in Paul's case it was probably melancholy. This is suggested by his brilliant mental gifts, as reflected primarily by his writings. Unlike many melancholy theologians who followed him, however, Paul's writings were highly practical, suggesting that his choleric temperament predominated. Temperaments that are basically melancholy, as we shall see, are usually more theoretical or philosophical and border on being impractical.

From the passages already examined, we can deduce several distinctly choleric tendencies in Saul of Tarsus. He was a leader by natural instinct, he was very zealous and activity prone, he was an angry, hostile, bitter individual, "breathing out threatening and slaughter." In addition, he was ruthless and cruel. In all probability, Saul of Tarsus would have been a great leader whether or not he became a Christian. His encounter with Jesus Christ on the Damascus road changed the direction of his leadership but did not lessen it. In fact, the Holy Spirit used this leadership ability as a dynamic force to glorify Jesus Christ. It is important to keep in mind that God does not obliterate temperament when we are Spirit filled, for each person retains his distinctive individualism. Instead, the Holy Spirit redirects our strengths to glorifying God and tempers our weaknesses by overcoming them with the characteristics of the Spirit-filled man. Saul-turned-Paul became a classic example of the Spirit-controlled choleric temperament.

Strong-willed

One of the best assets of a Choleric's temperament is his strong willpower. If pointed in the right direction, it makes him a most successful person. As a rule, Cholerics are successful in any vocation they select, but not because they have more mental gifts than other temperaments. Their success can be attributed to determination rather than native ability. When others have abandoned some endeavor or project, Mr. Choleric continues tenaciously until he reaches his goal. The Apostle Paul refers to this in 1 Corinthians 9:24-27 when describing standards of self-discipline.

"Know ye not that they who run in a race run all, but one

receiveth the prize? So run, that ye may obtain. And every man that striveth for the mastery is temperate in all things. Now they do it to obtain a corruptible crown, but we, an incorruptible. I, therefore, so run, not as uncertainly; so fight I, not as one that beateth the air. But I keep under my body, and bring it into subjection, lest that by any means, when I have preached to others, I myself should be a castaway."

This text gives us several insights into the strength of will of the choleric apostle. He indicates that he was "temperate in all things." His activity was not that of the Sanguine, who needs no purpose to satisfy him because the sheer joy of being active is sufficient satisfaction. The choleric apostle ran "not as uncertainly," indicating that he knew where he was, where he had been and where he was going; everything he did had purpose and meaning. He also indicates here that he did not abuse his body: "I keep under my body, and bring it into subjection." One can scarcely imagine the Apostle Paul being obese or intemperate even in today's affluent society.

It is the same choleric apostle who revealed an important secret from his personal life on how to live victoriously over weaknesses. He knew that self-discipline begins in the mind. If you don't determine in your mind to do something hard, it probably will not get done. In 2 Corinthians 10, Paul describes the spiritual power residing in the Christian's "flesh," meaning the body, that is "bringing into captivity every thought to the obedience of Christ." The disciplined Christian has a good purpose in his mind which produces positive feelings in his heart. This is very important, for the Lord Jesus said, "As a man thinketh in his heart, so is he." Success in the Christian life begins in the mind, and that is shaped by the will. If you indulge your weaknesses, excusing them and pampering yourself, you will not change. Only by acting on the truth that "I can do all things through Christ who strengtheneth me" will you be victorious in the warfare of the temperament (Philippians 4:13).

This strong willpower made the choleric apostle a very dynamic and exciting person. He was decisive and highly motivated, possessing the ability to lead and motivate others. He was seemingly indefatigable and full of faith. Strong will-power, however, has some subtle weaknesses and dangers. Many times a Christian Choleric is considered a great man of faith when in reality his faith is an exaggerated form of self-confidence. One of Mr. Choleric's greatest difficulties is, to trust in the Lord and not in his choleric temperament. He must remember that success is not by his might nor his power, but "by my Spirit, saith the Lord." Paul had a very acute awareness of his need for divine resources.

The hallmark of the choleric apostle — his persistence — is an admirable characteristic when directed by the Holy Spirit. But persistence can also get a choleric Christian far out of the will of God. Although some of my respected Christian friends tend to think the Apostle Paul revealed no grievous fault after his conversion, I believe the Bible relates an incident of his misguided persistence.

Toward the close of Paul's third missionary journey, recorded in Acts 20, he decided "if it were possible for him, to be at Jerusalem the day of Pentecost." We have no indication that this was of the Holy Spirit. It was a strong desire and a doubtful goal, but it grew to become a resolute, driving desire. Instead of visiting the church at Ephesus, he invited the elders to meet him in Miletus. Verse 22 says he was "bound in the spirit to go unto Jerusalem." This was Paul's spirit, indicating his determination to get to Jerusalem. We do not find that he asked the Lord about this, but arranged his plans according to his wishes.

This story indicates that even a mature Christian can get himself out of the will of God by setting his will above God's. Verse 23 shows that Paul had already been warned of unpleasant consequences, for "the Holy Spirit witnesseth in every city, saying that bonds and afflictions await me." But Paul would not be deterred, for he said, "But none of these things move me, neither count I my life dear unto myself, so that I might finish my course with joy, and the ministry, which I have received of the Lord Jesus. . . ."

The Lord wanted Paul to finish his course joyfully, but the time and place had not been revealed to Paul. If God wanted Paul to go to Jerusalem, his grace would assure it, not Paul's determination. Whether or not Paul actually got out of God's will by going to Jerusalem is a subject upon which I would not be dogmatic, although I personally think he did. But there is no question that his attitude was that of the flesh, not of the Spirit. Sometimes I think Christians have a tendency to lose much spiritual enjoyment, not because they do the wrong thing, but because they do it in the wrong way. That is, they set their minds on something, but they don't ask God because they're afraid he will say "no," so they just proceed on their own. Even though things may work out in the end, we may certainly wonder if such people wouldn't be much happier if they would heed the admonition, "In all thy ways acknowledge him, and he shall direct thy paths," instead of arching their choleric backs and setting their stubborn jaws to follow their own wills.

The Holy Spirit certainly revealed his will to Paul concerning the trip to Jerusalem, for the 21st chapter indicates that when he had come to Tyre, the Holy Spirit warned him through the disciples "that he should not go up to Jerusalem." But again Paul steadfastly persisted. A few days later, after arriving at Caesarea, they stayed in the home of Philip the evangelist. A Judean prophet named Agabus came and, taking Paul's belt, bound his hands and feet, saying, "Thus saith the Holy Spirit, So shall the Jews at Jerusalem bind the man that owneth this belt, and shall deliver him into the hands of the Gentiles." When the believers heard this they "besought him not to go up to Jerusalem." But Paul refused to heed their warnings. The Scripture tells us, "When he would not be persuaded, we ceased, saying, The will of the Lord be done." Either all these disciples and prophets were wrong or Paul was wrong. Hard-headed, self-willed Cholerics need to learn that when spiritually motivated people recommend a change in direction, they had better seek the will of the Holy Spirit on the matter. This is difficult for Cholerics because they thrive on opposi tion. The more we oppose a Choleric and attempt to hinder his activities, the more he lowers his shoulder and pushes.

A Christian doctor analytically described two different reactions to opposition shown by two minister friends of his. When the sanguine minister was opposed or threatened, he wanted to "take the threatener out for a cup of coffee and have fellowship with him." His insecurity made him want to use his charismatic gifts in charming his opposition into a spirit of cooperation. But the choleric minister reacted to opposition by "pushing that much harder."

The besetting temptation of choleric Christians is to set their minds on doing something and persistently push without knowing whether or not it is really the will of God. This may produce a seemingly productive Christian worker, but it does not make a happy Christian, nor does it make the best use of his talents. A Spirit-filled Choleric will always out-perform a carnal Choleric. Like every other temperament, Mr. Choleric desperately needs the filling of the Holy Spirit. To be otherwise is to incur many unnecessary difficulties, as did the Apostle Paul.

It is well known what happened to the choleric apostle who, more choleric than apostle, refused the admonitions of the Holy Spirit and went up to Jerusalem anyway. One sin leads to another, and we find Paul shaving his head and taking an Israelite vow in an attempt to please the Jews. Ordinarily compromise is not a temptation to Cholerics, but they are vulnerable to compromise when they think they may do a little thing wrong to do a big thing right. This may have been the apostle's thinking when he went up to Jerusalem and observed this Jewish custom, for he had a tremendous burden on his heart to reach the Jews.

God had called Paul to a great ministry among the Gentiles, which he fulfilled, but Paul's nationalistic spirit gave him a great burden for his own people, which is understandable and commendable. No doubt he thought that if he went through this Jewish rite, which to him was meaningless, it would put him in good with the Jews of Jerusalem so that he could preach the gospel to them. He learned — and all Christians should learn from this experience, recorded in Acts 21 and 22 — that it is never right to do wrong to get a chance to do right. It is always wrong to do wrong! In reality, disobedience is a form of unbelief, a lack of trust that if God wants us to preach in Jerusalem or witness to a great crowd or to a certain person, he can work it out. God is able to use the wrath of men to praise him; he does not need our sin to reveal his grace.

The choleric apostle paid dearly for his brief period of self-will. He was incarcerated in Jerusalem and then transferred to Caesarea, where he remained for approximately two years. He learned a valuable lesson through this personal experience from which all Christian Cholerics may profit: to turn their strong will over to God, who makes no mistakes in the direction of their lives.

This period of self-will must have been confessed, although Scripture does not indicate so, for we find that Paul goes on after this period of stumbling and is again very productive and usable in the hands of the Spirit of God. As we saw in the life of Sanguine Peter, we now see in the life of the choleric apostle that God does not carry a grudge, even when we sin. For God went on to use this man mightily in prison as a witness to governors, kings, and finally to Caesar himself. Many of Paul's epistles were written after this display of flesh-dominated temperament. Reinstatement with God is an instant experience for any believer who acknowledges his sin and yields himself again to God.

Hostile

The hostility and anger that characterizes the choleric temperament is not very apparent in the life of the Apostle Paul after his conversion. We have seen it motivate him prior to his conversion, but after his conversion it rarely appears. One such case is recorded in the 15th chapter of Acts at the outset of the second missionary journey. It seems that Paul and Barnabas had taken young John Mark, a nephew to Barnabas, with them on their first journey, but he turned back when they came to Perga (Acts 13:13). For that reason Paul was determined that Mark would not accompany them on their second journey. A Choleric could not tolerate quitters. By nature he would be intolerant of those who did not share his stamina and fortitude in the face of adversity. But Melancholy-Phlegmatic Barnabas insisted that his nephew join them. This is typical of his temperament for he was a loyal friend, a sacrificing individual who would be prone to give the lad another chance.

Paul was absolutely inflexible. Verse 39 indicates that "the contention was so sharp between them that they departed asunder one from the other; and so Barnabas took Mark, and sailed unto Cyprus." Some Christians like to pass this off as a wonderful way for the Holy Spirit to get two missionary journeys started instead of one, but that is aside from the real point. The Holy Spirit doesn't need an argument between brothers to accomplish his will. When Spirit-filled, we are not contentious, angry, hostile, and unforgiving. It may not have been God's will for Barnabas and Paul to leave on this trip together, for certainly he blessed the second journey and Paul's new companion, Silas. But we can be certain that the Holy Spirit did not need a typically choleric explosion by the Apostle Paul to precipitate such a decision.

Another eruption of the choleric apostle's anger is found in the 23rd chapter of Acts. Paul had been arrested and taken before the Sanhedrin council. He had just begun his defense speech, "I have lived in all good conscience before God until this day," when the high priest, Ananias, commanded the men who stood by Paul to "smite him on the mouth." Paul's instinctive reaction was to retort: "God shall smite thee, thou whited wall; for sittest thou to judge me after the law, and commandest me to be smitten contrary to the law?" Now it is true that Paul apologized when he realized he had reviled the high priest, but his outburst against injustice was the spontaneous expression of choleric hostility.

This episode is not repeated here to discredit the great apostle, but to show that a Christian Choleric has a problem with anger. He does not have to be dominated by it, for he can have victory over anger through the power of the Holy Spirit whenever he is willing to face it as a sin, confess it, and ask God to remove it. And he must repeat this action whenever he gets angry. When, like the Apostle Paul, he acts in self-will, he is vulnerable to the resurrection of the flesh. This can only be remedied by walking in the Spirit. Happy is the Choleric (and those around him) who is willing to label his anger immediately as sin, refuse the temptation to excuse it, and ask God to give him the peace of the Spirit-filled life.

Self-sufficient

As a result of his strong willpower, Mr. Choleric is very self-sufficient and independent. The more successful he becomes, the more his self-sufficiency will reveal itself. The self-sufficiency of the choleric apostle is seen in the fact that he refused payment for his Christian work though he acknowledged it was right and permissible to be paid. Whenever he went into a town or city to serve, he would ply his trade as a tent-maker (20.34). There is nothing wrong with a man's earning his own way, but this is a typical choleric reaction. Seldom is a Choleric found on the welfare rolls. In this instance I am reminded of my father, who had no small supply of choleric temperament. During the days of the great depression it was impossible for him to secure a job. Not only was his talent for machine repair useless to closed automobile plants, his handicap of having only one leg made finding employment more difficult. During the ten months we were on city welfare, my father refused to take the money unless he could work for it. The welfare agency let him deliver government food to welfare recipients who had no transportation, and then he accepted help.

Because of this feeling of independence and self-sufficiency, Mr. Choleric is not afraid to be alone; in fact, he is often called "a loner." It's not that he dislikes other people, but many times he would just rather do things by himself. This trait is seen in the Apostle Paul, who found himself alone in the city of Athens, a skeptical community filled with idolatry. Most people would sink into obscurity and wait until reinforcements arrived — but not the Apostle Paul. Acts 17 indicates that his heart burned so fiercely at the Athenians' plight that he entered into debates with the people, and when a crowd gathered he was brought to the Areopagus on Mars' hill to address the elite of the city.

I have been to Athens and have seen the ruins of the Acropolis, a magnificent center of pagan worship when Paul was there. Slight of stature at best, Paul must have looked minuscule beside the towering rock structures of the Acropolis as he declared the truth about the "unknown God." Undaunted by his lonely position, the choleric apostle proclaimed what is considered a classic example of pulpit oratory. Although the hearers' response was not overwhelming, the Scripture says: "Nevertheless, certain men joined him, and believed . . ." (Acts 17:34).

The spirit of self-sufficiency and independence may limit the effectiveness of the Christian Choleric because he does not readily sense the need for a personal devotional relationship to God and dependence on the ministry of the Holy Spirit. He is often so effective and capable in his own right that the plaudits of people fan his ego and he is tempted to proceed in Christian work without the power of God. Only when Mr. Choleric recognizes his utter uselessness without the Holy Spirit can he summon his strong willpower to a disciplined devotional life that produces a power-filled servant of God.

Choleric Saul's conversion is typical of the extreme measures that are often necessary to force the adult Choleric to humble himself and receive Jesus Christ. We do not know for certain that Paul had heard the gospel prior to Stephen's sermon; however, it seems likely that he had gained some knowledge of what was taught in order to have developed the intense hatred that led him to persecute the Christians. This is implied also by our Lord when he said to Paul: "It is hard for thee to kick against the pricks," indicating that he had been under conviction for some time. Choleric-induced self-sufficiency seems to provide amazing stamina and resistance against the conviction of the Holy Spirit in adult Cholerics. The late Henrietta C. Mears, one of the finest Christian educators of our time, used to say, "Never let a junior out of the department who doesn't know Jesus Christ." She knew that many boys, especially Cholerics, who do not know Christ by the time they finish the sixth grade, are not likely to respond to the Savior until the complexities of life drive them to their knees. That may explain the extreme measures the Lord took in sending a "light from heaven," blinding Paul, and then speaking to him audibly (Acts 9:1-8). Only when humbled by adversities will a Choleric respond to the gracious invitation to receive God's gift of eternal life.

Dynamic

Another characteristic of the choleric temperament that is apparent in the Apostle Paul is his native leadership ability. This was exhibited in his activities on the Jerusalem council, and it was also apparent on the first missionary journey. Barnabas and Paul comprised the first missionary team (Acts 13). Barnabas was the senior Christian who had invited Saul, the young convert, to work with him in the church at Antioch (Acts 11:25, 26). However, by the time they left the Isle of Cyprus, the group was designated "Paul and his company" (Acts 13:13), indicating that the reins of leadership had changed hands. From that point on it was "Paul and Barnabas." This leadership flashed on many occasions, one being when Paul and Silas confronted a young woman possessed with "a spirit of divination." "Paul, being grieved, turned and said to the spirit, I command thee, in the name of Jesus Christ, to come out of her. And he came out the same hour" (Acts 16:18). This aggressive leadership, obviously initiated by the Holy Spirit, is characteristic of this choleric apostle's ministry. Another illustration is found in Acts 27:21-25. Paul was a prisoner on board a ship bound for Rome. In the midst of a furious storm, the Roman guards were about to kill all their prisoners because of the Roman custom that required a guard to pay the price of the prisoners who escaped. Paul said: "Sirs, ye should have hearkened unto me, and not have loosed from Crete, and to have gained this harm and loss. And now I exhort you to be of good cheer; for there shall be no loss of any man's life among you, but only of the ship. For there stood by me this night an angel of God, whose I am, and whom I serve, saying, Fear not, Paul, thou must be brought before Caesar; and, lo, God hath given thee all them that sail with thee. Wherefore, sirs, be of good cheer; for I believe God, that it shall be even as it was told me." Only a Spirit-filled Choleric could react like this! The prisoner assumed authority of his captor's ship and saved their lives. This was more than an intuitive response to a challenging situation; it was supernaturally induced confidence from God.

Such boldness characterized the apostle all his life. He is perhaps the boldest witness recorded in the annals of the Church. Acts 22 relates how he boldly proclaimed his relationship to Jesus Christ in the face of Christ-hating Jews in Jerusalem who interrupted his sermon in a fit of anger and created a riot that was squelched only by the presence of the chief captain of the Romans. As a prisoner, Paul forthrightly defended himself before Tertullus, the governor; before Felix, who replaced Tertullus; and before Agrippa, king of the Herodians. In each case he personally challenged the king or governor with his message. Paul was a powerful preacher of the Word of God.

A thrilling illustration of the choleric apostle's bold witness occurred when, as a prisoner in Rome, he witnessed constantly to his captors and anyone else who would give him a hearing. In Philippians 4:22, while sending greetings to the church of Philippi, he stated, "All the saints greet you, chiefly they that are of Caesar's household." We could well ask how some of Caesar's household were made saints. Since all saints are fashioned through the hearing and receiving of the gospel, we perhaps can assume that some were converted through Roman soldiers who were chained to Paul during his imprisonment in Rome. While awaiting trial a prisoner customarily had a jailor chained to his wrist. One can scarcely imagine the Apostle Paul failing to boldly proclaim his faith to the guards. Such bold witness, inspired by the Holy Spirit, certainly brought fruit, perhaps in the very household of Caesar.

Practical

Cholerics as a rule have few aesthetic characteristics, but are highly practical. To them, life's decisions must be made with utilitarian purposes in view. That is one reason it is very difficult for a Choleric to relax and enjoy leisure time with his family. Many a modern Choleric is willing to work his fingers to the bone and provide the very best material benefits for his family, whereas the thing they desire most is his love, expressed by the time he spends with them.

The writings of the Apostle Paul abound in practical comments, as you will see by reading the last two or three chapters of Paul's epistles. His letters usually follow a pattern of doctrinal instruction in the first portion, answers to questions believers may have asked, and practical exhortation at the end. My color coding system for marking my Bible uses orange to indicate commands, and the last chapters of Paul's epistles are almost covered with orange. These commands have highly practical implications for the believer.

It is not difficult to pick out a choleric preacher, because his sermons abound in practical implications. Melancholy preachers are prone to emphasize theology and deal in the abstract. Sanguine preachers are known for their oratory and emotion. We happen to live in a day tuned to the practical side of life, and this may explain why most of the growing churches across the country are pastored by Cholerics. There are some noteworthy exceptions, but people readily gravitate to the man who teaches the Word of God in simple terms with practical applications to life.

The practical characteristics of choleric preachers may make them longer-winded than others. They frequently get by with it because they talk rapidly and maintain sufficient interest so that even self-indulgent Christians will sit through their lengthy sermons. This inclination makes them "compulsive communicators" because they know from the practical point of view that the gospel alone will solve the problems of mankind.

Such must have been the motivation of the Apostle Paul in Troas on his third missionary journey. On Sunday, when the disciples gathered together to break bread, "Paul preached unto them, ready to depart on the next day, and continued his speech until midnight" (Acts 20:7). Since Sunday was probably a work day, they may have met in the early evening and Paul preached four or five hours. A man named Eutychus, we're told, dozed off "and fell down from the third loft, and was taken up dead." The choleric apostle, undaunted by this tragedy, "went down, and fell on him, and embracing him said, Trouble not yourselves; for his life is in him." Preaching this man "to death" did not stop the compulsive, communicating choleric apostle! Instead, he went right back to preaching: "When he, therefore, was come up again, and had broken bread, and eaten, and talked a long while, even till break of day, so he departed."

One of the leaders in our church rather facetiously — though perhaps seriously — suggested that my sermon the previous Sunday night had been quite lengthy. My wife also clocked me at one hour and ten minutes, which was unusual for me. I responded, "I'm not as bad as the Apostle Paul; I've never killed anyone with my preaching." My friend wisely replied, "Pastor, when you can do what Paul did after he killed him through preaching, then you can preach that long too." Paul was obviously not just a choleric apostle, but a Spirit-filled Choleric with a deep desire to teach the truths of God to people he would never see again on this earth.

Crusading

Cholerics are born crusaders. They are the first in any community to instigate reform movements. When they observe social injustice, they are not just concerned, they immediately respond, "Let's get organized and do something about this." After observing Cholerics for many years, I concluded their crusades are not motivated so much by compassionate feelings as by their penchant for action. Usually the crusading Choleric is a tough-skinned individual, impervious to the opinions and feelings of others. He is the one temperament type who really doesn't care what other people think. This tendency becomes more pronounced as time goes on, particularly if he experiences a degree of success in his field. Christian Cholerics are prone to decide what is right and proceed to do it regardless of whose toes they step on or whom they offend. This can be a commendable trait if it is motivated by the right power, but sometimes it is a self-indulgence made to appear Christian.

Galatians 2 gives us an insight into the crusading, tough-skinned conduct of the choleric apostle. We saw this same experience earlier from the viewpoint of Sanguine Peter, who fellowshiped with the Gentiles until the Christian Jews arrived from Judea. Then, for fear of offending them, he separated himself from his Gentile brethren and their ways. The fact that Paul was among the youngest of the believers, that he was in the presence of the Church's leaders, and that his words would be closely examined did not deter the choleric apostle from taking action. Noting that the Gentile believers were affronted by Peter in a way contrary to the "truth of the gospel," Paul "withstood him to the face, because he was to be blamed." Paul further stated that he did this "before them all, saying, If thou, being a Jew, livest after the manner of Gentiles, and not as do the Jews, why compellest thou the Gentiles to live as do the Jews?" The fact that he might be ridiculed or in some other way rebuked by these "elders" was immaterial to Paul. He saw an injustice and he was moved to rectify it.

I cannot help but feel that the "great cloud of witnesses," who have a better understanding of truth since they have gone on to be with the Lord, were cheering Paul on. Most Christians in such circumstances are prone to keep their mouths sealed when rebuke is needed or to go away and criticize behind a person's back. It is always best to be straightforward with brethren in Christ. We often do more good to our brethren in rebuke than in silence. Naturally, care must be taken that our action is motivated by the Holy Spirit and not our selfish nature.

Controversial

Anyone with an abundance of choleric temperament is bound to be controversial, even when filled with the Holy Spirit. When Spirit-filled, he will be controversial for righteousness' sake; when he walks in the flesh, he will be controversial because of his choleric qualities. Everywhere Paul went, he was controversial. People either loved him or hated him. The zealous Jews, of course, hated him. A delegation would follow him from one city to another to stir up trouble and persecute him. They stoned him and left him for dead in Iconium. Some Jews in Jerusalem so hated Paul that their conduct was irrational. One group banded together and made a vow that they would neither eat nor drink until they had killed him.

All the reaction to the choleric apostle, however, was not hostility. He also motivated people to an intense feeling of love and loyalty. For instance, Timothy and Luke followed him halfway around the world.

Those who loved the Lord and were filled with the Spirit seemed to love Paul fervently. Throughout the book of Acts we find people who wept when he left town. This man who moved across the Middle East and southern Europe, leading thousands of people to a saving knowledge of Jesus Christ, is probably one of the most loved men in all of Christendom. Those who hated him did so because he was a powerful Christian.

Don't expect everyone to love you if you walk in the Spirit, but profit by the attitude of the Spirit-filled choleric apostle who was determined to please God, not man. A greater than the Apostle Paul was hated for righteousness — the Lord

Jesus Christ. If he could not please mankind, don't expect that you will. However, if you find yourself abrasive among Christians, you had better take stock to see whether your choleric traits are overriding the Spirit or the Spirit is truly controlling your temperament.

Paul's motivation

The choleric apostle was probably the world's most optimistic human being. That optimism produced the motivation that is unsurpassed in the history of the Church. Without access to human resources, the choleric apostle optimistically set out for parts unknown with only the assurance that the Spirit of God had sent him. He went through more suffering than any man known in church history. In 2 Corinthians 11 the apostle gives a report of some of his sufferings as a servant of Jesus Christ.

". . . In stripes above measure, in prisons more frequently, in deaths often. Of the Jews five times received I forty stripes, save one. Thrice was I beaten with rods, once was I stoned, thrice I suffered shipwreck, a night and a day I have been in the deep; in journeyings often, in perils of waters, in perils of robbers, in perils by mine own countrymen, in perils by the Gentiles, in perils in the city, in perils in the wilderness, in perils in the sea, in perils among false brethren; in weariness and painfulness, in watchings often, in hunger and thirst, in fastings often, in cold and nakedness. Beside those things that are without, that which cometh upon me daily, the care of all the churches." This is not a complete listing of the sufferings of Paul, for it was given long before his imprisonment in Jerusalem and subsequent shipwreck in the Mediterranean Sea en route to Rome. Little did he know when he wrote these words that he would be in prison at least three more times.

Humanly speaking, the natural temptation in adversity is to give up. Not so the Spirit-filled choleric apostle. Probably the best illustration of his optimism is seen after he was stoned and left for dead at Iconium on the first missionary journey (Acts 14:19-21). Most Christians would have fled to their homeland and never again embarked on a ministry to such ungrateful heathen. We sometimes read the words glibly: ". . . having stoned Paul, drew him out of the city, supposing he had been dead," and give little thought to the deep suffering of the apostle. We are not sure God brought Paul back from death, but the antagonists quit stoning him because they thought he was dead, so at least he was near death. This meant he suffered severe lacerations, bruises, and possibly broken bones. But instead of quitting, he "rose up, and came into the city; and the next day he departed with Barnabas to Derbe. And when they had preached the gospel in that city, and had taught many, they returned again to Lystra." What could possibly motivate a man to rise up from a rock pile of death, proceed to preach the gospel in Derbe, and shortly come back to Lystra and the rock throwers again? There is no human explanation, but there is a scriptural one. Paul had found the secret of motivation that many depressed and apathetic people of our society have failed to discover. The Old Testament tells us, "Where there is no vision, the people perish" (Proverbs 29:18). No man can be motivated without a vision. That is the reason a basically well-adjusted human being can lose all interest in life. Because changes come in life, he may realize a goal too soon or find that a goal is impossible. If he does not set another goal, he will ultimately waste away. Optimistic people continually maintain goals.

The choleric apostle's secret of motivation was given him by the Holy Spirit. He revealed it to the church of Philippi in the third chapter, verses 13 and 14, where he acknowledged that, although he was not perfect, he had learned to do one thing: "Forgetting those things which are behind, and reaching forth unto those things which are before, I press toward the mark for the prize of the high calling of God in Christ Jesus."

The Apostle Paul could forget the stonings, shipwrecks, hunger, beatings, and rejection by men because he didn't look back; instead, he always looked forward to the ultimate goal when he would stand before Jesus Christ to give an account of himself. Next to the filling of the Holy Spirit, that is the greatest secret of motivation in the world. Actually, the two go hand in hand.

Whenever a Christian mopes, gripes, and feels sorry for himself, he is looking back to personal affronts, deprivations, sufferings, or rebukes. That is never productive, healthful, or helpful to the Christian. In fact, it is deeply demoralizing. The Apostle Paul, like Abraham before him, looked for a city whose builder and maker is God. He looked especially for the Savior and lived his life under the motivation that Jesus Christ was coming back, when he wanted to hear Jesus say, "Well done, thou good and faithful servant."

If you are an unmotivated, frustrated, ineffective Christian, I suggest that in addition to checking your life for habits that grieve the Spirit of God, you should also examine your goals. Man is a goal-striving being; if he has no goal he does not strive. Have you ever noticed how on a day off work you have little motivation unless you are going somewhere or doing something special? The anticipation of engaging in a specific project motivates you.

Extensive experiments on motivation show that "as a man thinketh in his heart, so is he," and particularly at night. If you want to be motivated tomorrow, go to bed tonight thinking positively and optimistically about what God is going to do with and through you tomorrow. Think specifically, anticipating what you expect God to do and how you expect to face challenges and opportunities. Evangelist John Hunter has said, "Christians do not have problems when they face the issues of life, but if they do not face them in faith, they become problems." The night before your day off, sit down and write out a list of all the things you want to accomplish the next day, placing the items in an order of priority. Then pray about it. You will be amazed how much easier it is to awaken the next day, how much happier you will feel during the day, and how satisfied you will go to bed. But if you retire thinking how tired you are, you are likely to be tired the next morning.

During the past two years I have been experimenting with

this, primarily because I have been preaching as many as five sermons on Sunday, three in the morning and two in the evening. At the close of the first Sunday on that schedule I was completely exhausted and could scarcely pull my feet into bed at the end of the day. The last thing I said to my wife was, "Don't wake me; I'm just going to sleep until I wake up." I slept until 10:30 the next morning and was absolutely miserable when I awakened. For weeks I kidded myself that I needed Monday to "recuperate from Sunday's preaching schedule." Each Sunday night I programmed into my brain the fact that I was completely exhausted and I would relax and recuperate the next day. It didn't take my wife long to get me out of the habit of sleeping until 10:30, but she couldn't get me into a good mood on Monday.

Fortunately, the Lord took care of it, because with the resignation of a Bible teacher in our Christian high school, I agreed to teach the early morning Bible class in his place, forgetting that the class met the first thing Monday morning. Once having committed myself to the responsibility, I wasn't about to turn back. As I crawled into bed Sunday night after preaching five times, I studied my Bible in preparation for teaching the young people the next morning. To my amazement, Mr. Lethargy turned into Mr. Vitality. As I watched myself carefully through the next few months, I found that my attitude at night determined how I awakened the next day. We had an off-Monday from school two months later, and again I awakened feeling miserable. That's when the Holy Spirit revealed to me that for years as a minister I had pampered myself into thinking that I had to take a day off Monday in order to recuperate from Sunday. My wife and I had a family conference, and we decided that since our children were teen-agers and out of the home five days a week at school, I should quit taking Monday off and choose Saturday as my day for maximum sharing with the family. For over two years now I have been enjoying a highly motivated work schedule on Mondays in direct proportion to my mental optimism on Sunday night.

The Apostle Paul, of course, had far greater goals than these. He dragged his tired, aching body from Iconium because the city of Derbe was desperately in need of the gospel of Jesus Christ. That was the short-range goal which motivated him to walk those weary miles to the next harvest field. If you would be a motivated, Spirit-filled Christian, ask the Spirit of God to give you short-range, medium-range, and long-range goals. You will complete the short-range and medium-range in this life, but only when we stand before the Lord Jesus will we reach the eternal goal he has set for the child of God.

A lack of goal-setting accounts for the early deaths of many retired people. Although a man can be very productive in his field with the ultimate goal of retirement at sixty-five, he may die before his retirement is two years along. It may not be poor health that kills him, but poor "vision." As long as the goal of relaxing and retiring is ahead, he has something to work for. But after the novelty of relaxed living wears off, he is left without any specific purpose and consequently declines in energy. Unless a retired person is able to program a new goal and a new vision for leisure hours, he will shorten his life.

I mention this in the midst of the study of the choleric apostle, who "died with his boots on," because many Christians get to the age of maximum opportunity to serve Jesus Christ and then decide to retire. I have seen people in their late forties, with their children married or off to college, drop all forms of Christian service, much to their own loss. No Christian is going to be happy and confident unless his life is consistently available to the Holy Spirit.

A lady once asked me, "What is the age of retirement from Christian service?" I replied, "There is none!" As long as there is one sinner in this world and one Christian to convey the message of Christ to him, that Christian has no right to retire. Any pastor will tell you that the most disgruntled, cantankerous, unhappy people are elderly Christians who have no purpose in life. The happiest senior Christians I have met are those who constantly invest themselves in the service of our Lord and Savior.

When my wife and I were in Hong Kong several years ago, we took a tour of the Oriental Boat Mission's "field" in the Hong Kong harbor. There we met the most motivated and interesting octogenarian I have ever seen. She was an 82-year-old missionary from England whose board had said she was too old to return to the field. After being forced into retirement, she decided that God had called her to the mission field for life, so under his orders she went out again, depending on him for support. This dear lady was actively engaged in the thing she enjoyed best, sharing Jesus Christ with the refugees from Red China who, possessing no homes, lived in rickshaws or in Chinese junks tied together and docked in the harbor. After a lifetime of motivation this saint of God could say with the apostle, "I have fought a good fight, I have finished my course, I have kept the faith; henceforth there is laid up for me a crown of righteousness, which the Lord, the righteous judge, shall give me at that day; and not to me only, but unto all them also that love his appearing" (2 Timothy 4:7, 8).

What was her secret? Like the apostle, she had a lifetime goal: "the prize of the high calling of God in Christ Jesus," for which she was actively striving. What is your goal? The quality and definiteness of your goal will determine your motivation. The Holy Spirit has a goal for every Christian; let him motivate you.

Paul's transformation

Much of the Holy Spirit's transformation of the choleric apostle's temperament had to do with directing him in the way God wanted him to go. We shall now examine some of the characteristics of the Apostle Paul revealed in the Scripture that are completely contrary to the natural choleric temperament. Paul's instant obedience, after his conversion to Christ, is predictable, because Cholerics are prone to be decisive and act intuitively. But the humility that came into this haughty, aristocratic Pharisee's heart cannot be explained by natural means.

In spite of the potential effectiveness of the Choleric, he is probably by nature in need of more of the Spirit-filled characteristics than any of the other temperaments. Galatians 5:22, 23 reveals the following characteristics needed by the choleric temperament. All of them are found in the life of the Apostle Paul after his conversion.

Love. The first characteristic of the Spirit-filled life is love, which is probably the greatest single need of the choleric believer. By nature Cholerics are unfeeling, hard, unemotional individuals who find it very difficult to express love. Even when they do, it is often mistakenly directed into doing things for other people and expecting them to interpret that as a demonstration of love. Compassion is naturally foreign to a Choleric.

As we read the life of the Apostle Paul, we find him to be a loving Choleric. The Holy Spirit thrillingly transformed him from an angry, bitter, persecuting individual to a compassionate, warm-hearted person. He retained the strength of character and innate sternness of the Choleric, but he consistently conveyed the compassionate, loving interest in other people that is needed in an effective Christian.

There are many illustrations in Paul's writings and in the book of Acts to illustrate our point, but one will suffice. In the book of Romans, the choleric apostle writes, "Brethren, my heart's desire and prayer to God for Israel is, that they might be saved" (10:1). "I say the truth in Christ, I lie not, my conscience also bearing me witness in the Holy Spirit, that I have great heaviness and continual sorrow in my heart. For I could wish that I myself were accursed of God for my brethren, my kinsmen according to the flesh" (9:1-3). No natural Choleric, knowing about eternal damnation and loss of heaven, would be willing to make the sacrifice Paul refers to here. He was actually declaring that he would exchange his place in heaven for hell if the nation Israel could be saved. The self-love of the Choleric renders this absolutely supernatural, possible only by the Holy Spirit. This compassion by the choleric apostle is not exceptional, for we also find it in his attitude toward entire churches, toward individuals, and even toward some of his enemies.

We have a right to expect that a Spirit-filled, choleric Christian will have a compassionate heart towards others. This compassion should begin in his own family and extend to his relatives, his neighbors, and to the most remote peoples of the earth.

It is from the experienced pen of the same choleric apostle that the Holy Spirit admonishes all believers to "rejoice in the Lord always, and again I say, Rejoice" (Philippians 4:4). He also instructed us, "See that none render evil for evil unto any man, but ever follow that which is good, both among yourselves, and to all men. Rejoice evermore. Pray without ceasing. In everything give thanks; for this is the will of God in Christ Jesus concerning you. Quench not the Spirit" (1 Thessalonians 5:15-19). More of God's people quench the Spirit of God by griping and chafing than by anything else. Paul, by example and commandment, admonishes us to "rejoice evermore," and in everything to give thanks — thus we fulfill the will of God. If you are not a rejoicing Christian, you are not a Spirit-filled Christian. Instead of griping and fuming over annoyances, get down on your knees and confess your thankless spirit or persecution complex to God as sin. Ask him to take it away and fill you with his Spirit, then the joy of the Lord will be your experience.

Sometimes we understand the dealings of God with his people; sometimes we do not. You will find when you come to one of those perplexing circumstances that you rejoice anyway. How? By faith through the Holy Spirit. When circumstances look bleak, remember that God is in control and we can rejoice by faith through the ministry of the Holy Spirit in us. Expressing our joy lifts us; expressing our gripes depresses us. It is God's will that we rejoice both in the things we understand and the things we do not. Obedience to this one command will tremendously exhilarate and purify our emotional life.

Peace. Peace in heart is foreign to the carnal Choleric. Not only is he not at peace, but he resents others' having peace. The only sense of peace he experiences is absorption in whirlwind activities; the moment he stops, he is restless to be up and doing, envisioning and prodding something else.

We might expect that the highly motivated and aggressive choleric apostle would find peace only in action. But the record indicates otherwise. The Holy Spirit had so modified the Apostle Paul that he knew peace was not dependent on ideal circumstances. Happy is the Christian who recognizes that heart peace and outward circumstances need not be related. We have not experienced spiritual victory when peace of heart accompanies a pleasant situation. But when things are going wrong and we still have peace, the controlling presence of the Holy Spirit is bearing fruit. Such was the modified character of the choleric apostle.

Nothing could be worse for the dynamic preacher of the gospel than confinement and curtailment of his public ministry. A zealous preacher can bear almost any trial if he can regularly and effectively preach the Word of God. But when the Apostle Paul was imprisoned for proclaiming the gospel of Jesus Christ, a supernatural sense of peace invaded his being. It was this same choleric apostle who said, "Not that I speak in respect of want; for I have learned, in whatsoever state I am, therewith to be content. I know both how to be abased, and I know how to abound; everywhere and in all things I am instructed both to be full and to be hungry, both to abound and to suffer need" (Philippians 4:11, 12).

One day while visiting a discouraged church member confined to bed for a few weeks, I tried to lift her spirit by sharing Paul's challenge to rejoice evermore and experience peace of heart in spite of the circumstances. I read Paul's testimony, "I have learned in whatsoever state I am, therewith to be content," and she retorted, "Well, Paul had never been in a state like this!" I looked at this woman who knew nothing about suffering compared with the apostle, and asked, "Do you know where he was when he made that statement?" "No," she replied. "In jail, waiting to be brought before Caesar and possibly executed for the cause of Christ." Quite embarrassed, she admitted her impulsiveness and entered into prayer in a new spirit. If we chafe and fume in our circumstances, we cannot have the peace of God.

Some Christians fret and worry until they lose control of themselves. The Bible tells us, "Be anxious for nothing; but in everything by prayer and supplication with thanksgiving, let your request be made known unto God. And the peace of God, which passeth all understanding, shall keep your hearts and minds through Christ Jesus" (Philippians 4:6, 7). This statement also was made by the Holy Spirit through the pen of the Apostle Paul while he was in prison. If you lack peace and contentment, confess your self-centered bitterness or fear and ask the Spirit of God to give you his peace.

Gentleness. Carnal Cholerics, by nature, know nothing of gentleness — at least not in the sense the Bible means gentleness. Most translators indicate that the word means "kindness." Can you imagine a thick-skinned, hardnosed, square-jawed but gentle Choleric? Can you further imagine him as polite, gracious, and considerate, performing gentle acts of kindness for others? These stem from a compassionate, tender heart, and that comes only by the filling of the Holy Spirit.

The Apostle Paul exhibited all of these gentle characteristics. The book of Philemon was written as an expression of gentleness, pleading for the welfare of a fellow Christian. An evidence of spontaneous gentleness is recorded in the last written words of the choleric apostle. We have already seen how he blasted Barnabas for insisting on taking young John Mark on the second missionary journey, but in 2 Timothy 4:11 we find these words: "Take Mark, and bring him with thee; for he is profitable to me for the ministry." Paul was big enough to acknowledge that Mark had become a faithful servant of God. This same gentleness, motivated by compassion, is also seen in the apostle's treatment of women. By nature choleric men are not usually very thoughtful of women. And choleric women can be downright nasty to other women, almost as if they resent being women and are scornful of other women who lack their drive and initiative.

Christian Cholerics should go out of their way to be gentle to other people, particularly to women. The self-confidence of a Choleric often creates a feeling of inferiority or insecurity in others. Because he is usually quick of tongue and prone to be sharp and sarcastic, he tends to incite fear in others. From my experience in the counseling room, I would say that more Christian women married to Cholerics have suffered emotional shock than women married to the other three temperaments combined. This is quite understandable when Cholerics do not know Jesus Christ and are not filled with the Holy Spirit, but such mistreatment of the gentler sex is shameful in a Christian companion.

Cholerics tend to dominate every area of activity; consequently, they do not permit others to use their talents and gain self-confidence from personal achievement. Christian Cholerics would be wise to go out of their way to commend others and to show their approval in commendable things. I have observed that, as a rule, Cholerics are very hard to please. Since they are highly opinionated, they easily overlook good and show disapproval because of a minor failure. Yet approval and encouragement is necessary to enhance respect and love. When the Holy Spirit fills a Choleric's life, he will be more concerned about the feelings of others than in letting off steam or expressing himself; this is seen in his gentleness.

A most commendable treatment of women was exhibited by the Apostle Paul in the 16th chapter of Acts. He had been summoned to Macedonia by a man in a vision, but the first devout people he met there were women. At a women's prayer meeting he gave his first message in Europe, and the first convert was Lydia, a seller of rich linen. The entire story shows Paul's gentle concern and respect for womanhood, which was not only contrary to the custom of the day but also opposed to his choleric temperament. Men who are not gentle toward women in general, and their own wives in particular, are not Spirit-filled. The best solution to marital disharmony is the filling of the Holy Spirit. This benefit, of course, is not limited to the marriage relationship but is healing in any conflict arising between people.

Meekness. In his writing on the temperaments, theologian Alexander Whyte offers this prayer that should be the attitude of the choleric Christian: "Lord, let me be ever courteous, and easy to be entreated. Never let me fall into a peevish or contentious spirit. Let me follow peace with all men, offering forgiveness, inviting them by courtesies, ready to confess my own errors, apt to make amends, and desirous to be reconciled. Give me the spirit of a Christian, charitable, humble, merciful and meek, useful and liberal, angry at nothing but my own sins, and grieving for the sins of others, that, while my passion obeys my reason, and my reason is religious, and my religion is pure and undefiled, managed with humility, and adorned with charity, I may escape thy anger, which I have deserved, and may dwell in thy love, and be thy son and servant forever, through Jesus Christ our Lord, Amen."

Faith. Faith is another spiritual trait greatly needed by the carnal Choleric. Oh, he has plenty of faith in himself, which we call self-confidence, but he desperately needs to believe God and trust God for everything. The Apostle Paul is a classic example of a Spirit-filled Choleric who no longer trusts in himself but relies implicitly on the living God. One of many passages that reveals this is Paul's extraordinary statement spoken on a ship in the midst of a storm: "Sirs, be of good cheer; for I believe God, that it shall be even as it was told me" (Acts 27:25). This faith comes from knowing the Word of God and being controlled by the Holy Spirit. It is sometimes difficult to tell whether a choleric Christian is placing his faith in himself or in God. But he knows. If he is trusting in himself, he is not Spirit-filled.

Humility. Many passages in the book of Acts and in Paul's epistles reveal a surprising humility in a choleric temperament. One such passage is Acts 14 where Paul and Barnabas receive acclaim as gods by the people of Lystra. Immediately the apostles tore their clothes in revulsion and asserted that they were just human beings. Shortly after this Paul was stoned and left for dead, perhaps because some people were disillusioned or vengeful at discovering that the miracle-working men were only flesh and blood. Such an opportunity to masquerade as a god would have been seized and exploited by a carnal Choleric.

The Holy Spirit was aware of Paul's need for humility, for after his vision of heaven recorded in 2 Corinthians 12, he noted in verse 7: "And lest I should be exalted above measure through the abundance of the revelations, there was given to me a thorn in the flesh, the messenger of Satan to buffet me, lest I should be exalted above measure." Although Paul prayed that this "thorn" of affliction be removed, God promised his grace would be sufficient for Paul's need, and the thorn remained. This is an example of a Spirit-approved (and Satan-inspired!) physical adversity to maintain a Christian's humility and dependence on God. Since God never does anything not for good (Romans 8:28), we may conclude that Paul had a struggle with the trait of humility — as does every Choleric. Many a Christian Choleric is proud and domineering of his natural temperament. As he refuses to change, he perpetuates his spiritual immaturity and restricts God's use of his life.

Jacob Behman, as quoted by Alexander Whyte, made the following statement concerning the Choleric's need of humility. "That man, who has his soul compassed about with a choleric complexion, must above all things practice at every turn and exercise himself like an athlete in humility. He must everyday pour the cold water of humility on the hot coals of his own complexion. Take all thy might after meekness in word and thought, and so shall not thy temperament inflame thy soul. Choleric man, mortify thy temperament and thy complexion, and do all to the glory of God."

Who can doubt after reading 2 Corinthians and understanding the events that inspired it that the choleric apostle had learned to humble himself? When his own spiritual children rebuffed him and rejected his first epistle because he named their sin, he spoke endearingly, patiently, and graciously, without the sarcastic barbs that characterize the natural Choleric. This can only be attributed to the modifying ministry of the Holy Spirit.

When the Lord Jesus spoke to Paul from heaven and said, "I am Jesus, whom thou persecutest; it is hard for thee to kick against the goads," Paul instantly answered, "Lord, what wilt thou have me to do?" (Acts 9:5, 6). When the Lord instructed him to arise and go into the city, he immediately obeyed. From that point on, his life was characterized by prompt obedience, indicating his complete yieldedness to the Holy Spirit.

On the Damascus road Paul surrendered his strong choleric will to Jesus Christ. Only rarely did he retake that will from his Master. So he could counsel others in Romans 6:13, "Neither yield ye your members as instruments of unrighteousness unto sin, but yield yourselves unto God, as those that are alive from the dead, and your members as instruments of righteousness unto God."

God has given to every man a free will which he can use as he sees fit. Paul chose to reject self-will and its brittle potentialities, and accept the perfect will of Jesus Christ. We cannot imagine all that was involved in that instant decision. As a member of the select Sanhedrin, Saul the Pharisee had a glittering future. Starting out at such a young age on the council, he would likely have become a prominent leader of Israel and might have become the high priest. When he yielded himself to Jesus Christ he was in effect saying, "I am giving up all efforts for personal glory, all opportunities for personal power, and am turning my back on everything I previously worked for because it was all opposed to the will of Jesus Christ." There were no strings on Paul's commitment, but perfect yieldedness.

Some Christians think that such a decision is a great sacrifice. A young person may fear that if he surrenders his life to

Jesus Christ he will end up in a jungle wilderness or a position alien to his interests. This betrays a twisted conception of God's love. Our heavenly Father wants us to be happy more than we do. I have yet to meet a miserable Christian who is fully surrendered to God's will, but I know many frustrated Christians who will not yield their lives to God.

At the time Paul made his dynamic decision, it seemed as though he were giving up a great deal. He was unceremoniously expelled from the Sanhedrin council and his name became despised in Israel. But as the Apostle Paul he proceeded under the controlling power of the Holy Spirit to become the greatest name in Christian history. How many of the other Sanhedrin members can you remember? Most of the world knows about the choleric Apostle Paul. Certainly fame doesn't come through dedication to Christ, but personal fulfillment comes only in this way. Paul's life is a classic example of Jesus' words: "He that findeth his life shall lose it; and he that loses his life for my sake shall find it" (Matthew 10:39). What are you doing with your life? If it isn't yielded to the Lord Jesus Christ, I suggest that you give it to him and receive a hundredfold in return.

6

MOSES THE MELANCHOLY

The richest of all temperaments is the melancholy. It is usually blessed with a gifted mind and a tremendous capacity to experience the complete spectrum of emotions. Its greatest danger is in giving in to negative thinking patterns that exaggerate its pessimistic tendencies. Some of the world's greatest geniuses have been gifted Melancholies who squandered their talents in the slough of despondency and became apathetic and unproductive. This should never happen to a Christian Melancholy, for he has a source of power within him to change a negative thinking pattern to positive and motivate him to the maximum use of his talents. The secret of motivation is one's thinking pattern, and the key to a proper thinking pattern is the Spirit-filled life. A simple rule that will help a Christian Melancholy is to question the validity of every negative thought, counter it with positive thought, and claim Philippians 4:13. Amazing results will follow.

Evidence that melancholic Christians have abundant potential is seen in the lives of great men of God in the Bible who were more often melancholy than any other temperament. The Melancholies' "hall of fame" would include Jacob, Solomon, Elijah, Elisha, Jeremiah, Isaiah, Daniel, Ezekiel, Obadiah, Jonah, John the Baptist, the Apostles John and Thomas, and many others. Heading this list of famous servants of God is the greatest man in the history of Israel, Moses the Melancholy.

In order to evaluate the temperament of Moses we should first examine the strengths and weaknesses of the melancholy temperament. Mr. Melancholy is the most talented of all the temperaments. He is a natural perfectionist, very sensitive and appreciative of the fine arts, analytical, self-sacrificing, and a faithful friend. He is not outgoing as a rule and rarely pushes himself forward. With his exceptional gifts come equally complex weaknesses that often neutralize his effectiveness. He tends to be moody, critical, pessimistic, and self-centered. The world's great artists, composers, philosophers, inventors, and theoreticians have usually been Melancholies.

Melancholy Moses provides an excellent study in temperament analysis because so much information is given about him in Scripture. Certain factors, however, make it difficult to determine whether some activities were motivated by the power of God or the variations of his temperament. First, he lived before Pentecost when the Holy Spirit did not indwell believers as he does today. Even more important, a melancholy person experiences a variety of mood fluctuations that are sometimes confusing. It is easy to diagnose his dark moods as flesh motivated, but sometimes his bright moods make him appear Spirit-led when he is not. One can only determine his real source of control by his actions over a period of time.

The melancholy leader of Israel is a classic illustration of the difference which the power of God makes in a man's life. After forty years of education in the center of Egyptian culture, this brilliant Melancholy spent forty years tending animals in a remote desert. At eighty he heard God from a burning bush, and during the next forty years he was one of the greatest leaders in the history of the world. The change in this melancholy servant of Jehovah was gradual, sometimes sporadic, occasionally electrifying, but in some cases regressive. All of this establishes him as quite human and provides us with a typical illustration of Spirit-directed melancholy temperament when he was yielded to the Holy Spirit and raw melancholy temperament when he was not. Like any other Christian, Moses was productive for God only when he was controlled by the Holy Spirit.

Gifted

The inherent talent and gifts of Moses the Melancholy are apparent throughout the entire scriptural narrative. In Acts 7, Stephen, the first Christian martyr, informs us that Moses "was learned in all the wisdom of the Egyptians, and was mighty in words and in deeds" (Acts 7:22). Egypt was a leading center of civilization in Moses' day, apparently, and he absorbed the knowledge of the Egyptians without being dominated by it. The concepts of the Egyptians were heavily inculcated with superstition, none of which taints the writings of Moses. This is not only a testimony to his ability, but a confirmation of the power of the Holy Spirit within him as he wrote. The tremendous gifts of character and the Holy Spirit are graphically illustrated in his writings in the first five books of the Bible. Granted, the Holy Spirit gave these Scriptures to Moses, but the personality of Moses shines through the scriptural narrative, establishing him as the outstanding intellect of the Old Testament, just as the Apostle Paul's writings confirm him as the outstanding scholar among New Testament writers.

Melancholy people have a capacity for the dramatic and rise to great heights on occasion. Moses was never better cast than when he appeared before the Egyptian Pharaoh, unemotionally delivered the warning of God, and eventually convinced the stubborn king with ten miraculous plagues to let God's people go free. As a general rule, melancholy people excel under this kind of pressure because external motivation spurs their latent talents. Once the pressure is off, however, they tend to recede into apathy unless motivated by the Holy Spirit.

The ability of Moses to lead three million people on a wilderness journey and control them as judge, prophet, and mediator with God reflects his exceptionally gifted nature. Even acknowledging the special guidance of God and his divine enabling in his melancholy servant, we are confronted with a man of tremendous gifts. Secular historians agree that Moses was one of the superior men of his time.

Self-sacrificing

One of the hallmarks of a melancholy temperament is a desire to be self-sacrificing. Strongly melancholy individuals find it difficult to enjoy ease or success without a guilty conscience. They are often prone to dedicate themselves to some sacrificial cause. This usually is on a personal basis with a high personal cost. Dr. Albert Schweitzer was a good example of such a gifted, self-sacrificing temperament. He had already distinguished himself as an exceptional musician and able philosopher when he took up medicine and devoted his life to healing the sick in a remote area of Africa. Typical of his temperament, he chose an area where the people could never adequately compensate him for his services.

One of the values of a temperament study for Melancholies is its help for decision-making. Melancholies should carefully check their tendency to be "sacrificial" for selfish reasons! Sometimes they cramp and misdirect their lives in a self-sacrificing endeavor that actually is self-serving — a means of heightening pride through self-abasement. Some humanitarian enterprises are compensations for self-deficiencies, and therefore are not as noble as they appear. Service and sacrifice must not be disparaged, but the melancholy person should examine his decisions to see that they are God-directed, not self-centered.

Very little is known about the life of Moses between his adoption by Pharaoh's daughter and his identification with his own people forty years later. The book of Hebrews, however, reveals how Moses came to his crucial decision. "By faith Moses, when he was come to years, refused to be called the son of Pharaoh's daughter, choosing rather to suffer affliction with the people of God than to enjoy the pleasures of sin for a season, esteeming the reproach of Christ greater riches than the treasures in Egypt; for he had respect unto the recompense of the reward. By faith he forsook Egypt, not fearing the wrath of the king; for he endured, as seeing him who is invisible" (11:24-27).

Jewish historians suggest on the basis of tradition that Moses was the prime minister of Egypt and as the adopted son of Pharaoh's daughter he was second only to the Pharaoh himself. But he chose to "suffer affliction with the people of God" — a very self-sacrificing decision. We realize from this passage that Moses had the spiritual capacity to understand the transient value of this world and the enduring riches of the life to come. On that basis he was willing to sacrifice the "pleasures of sin for a season" that he might be God's man and earn an eternal reward.

To one degree or another, all Christians face this decision. It seems easier for a melancholy person to see through the sham and the shallow material rewards this world offers and to rightly evaluate eternal things. I have observed that many missionaries going to the foreign field have a higher-than-average degree of melancholy temperament. This characteristic accounts for the fact that many gifted missionaries are willing to renounce the pleasures and possessions of this life to serve Jesus Christ here and anticipate his "Well done, thou good and faithful servant," plus the reward that "fadeth not away, reserved in heaven for you." Moses' life proves that no man loses who gives his life to God.

Self-depreciating

Although the Melancholy may possess the greatest native talents of any of the temperaments, these talents are often neglected because of an inordinate feeling of inferiority. Melancholy people are perfectionists; consequently, they are rarely satisfied with anything they do or anyone else does because it fails to measure up to their high standards of perfection. It is almost impossible for a Melancholy who is unaided by the Holy Spirit to graciously receive commendation or congratulations. Whether directing an orchestra or quarterbacking a football team, he remembers his mistakes rather than the overall success.

A publisher and I discussed the writings of one of the great Bible scholars of our day who possesses no small degree of melancholy temperament. His work is so excellent that the published books instantly become outstanding sellers. Yet they reach the reader only after long delays. Printing deadlines have to be pushed back because the author constantly revises his work. The first draft of his writing looks eloquent to other people, but the gifted Melancholy is dissatisfied.

Parents must be especially considerate of this tendency in a melancholy child, for criticism makes a deep impression on his sensitive nature and may discourage further effort. When asked to undertake a project, the strong Melancholy activates his inferiority complex with a series of excuses. If he can be persuaded to try, he usually does an excellent job. When stripped of his excuses, Mr. Melancholy begins to realize that his reluctance stems from his self-protective instinct. His aversion to criticism — by himself or others — is greater than his desire to see the job done.

The excuses Moses gave to Almighty God during their conversation at the burning bush are a classic example of Melancholies' low esteem for themselves. We will look at each of them in detail to see how a gifted and sincere man can live far below his potential. Fortunately, Moses responded in spite of his excuses, and later events proved Moses could do what he thought he couldn't. A melancholy person should never trust his feelings to guide him through a door of opportunity for God. Instead, he should commit himself to God's sure leading. Then he can claim Philippians 4:13 and know that God will supply his needs, and remind himself that "If God be for us, who can be against us?" (Romans 8:31).

1. *I don't have any talent!* After appearing to Moses in the burning bush and revealing his long-range plan of leading the Jews out of Egypt and into "a land flowing with milk and honey," God said to Moses, "Come now therefore, and I will send thee unto Pharaoh, that thou mayest bring forth my people the children of Israel out of Egypt" (Exodus 3:10). Moses unfurled his inferiority complex by replying, "Who am

I, that I should go unto Pharaoh, and that I should bring forth the children of Israel out of Egypt?" In other words, Moses was protesting: "I don't have any talent." Though secretly proud, as a typical Melancholy, Moses depreciated his personal ability. So he shrank from making his talent available to God.

Many melancholy Christians do the same thing today. When challenged by a Sunday school superintendent or pastor, they draw back, thinking: "Who am I?" or "I don't have any talent." God's answer to Moses is as valid for twentieth-century Christians as for the chosen leader of Israel. God promised, "Certainly I will be with thee!" What more did Moses need!

Of tremendous help to every melancholy Christian would be a study in the Bible concerning God's provision. Reading through the Scriptures, we find that whether God is speaking to Adam and Eve, Noah, Abraham, Moses, the prophets, or the kings, he always promises to keep and strengthen them. And the Lord Jesus promised his disciples the same just before he left this world.

In Matthew 28:18-20, after issuing the Great Commission, which commanded believers to go into all the world and preach the gospel to every creature, Jesus concluded, ". . . and, lo, I am with you always, even unto the end of the age." What greater assurance could a Melancholy ask who is struggling with an inferiority complex? If you as a Christian Melancholy have a tendency to reject opportunities for Christian service, may I suggest that you remind yourself that God has promised, "Certainly I will be with thee!" Actually, since God indwells our lives in the person of his Holy Spirit, we don't even need talent to serve him — we simply need to be responsive to his directing.

2. *I don't know theology.* Melancholy Moses' second excuse for not serving God was as ill founded as the first. He assumed that when he went to lead Israel out of Egypt the people would question his commission from God, and so he weakly inquired, "What shall I say unto them?" Moses was trained in the arts of the Egyptians, but he was not yet in-

structed in the principles of God and he knew that many of the Israelites raised in the land of Goshen were educated in the faith of their fathers.

Many modern-day Christians claim ignorance as an excuse for failing to witness for Christ. Before they share what Jesus Christ has done for them, they imagine a skeptic concocting a philosophical or theological question they cannot cope with and so they refuse to try. Jesus prepared the seventy messengers of his kingdom by assuring them: "It shall be given you in that same hour what ye shall speak. For it is not ye that speak, but the Spirit of your Father who speaketh in you" (Matthew 10:19, 20).

The Lord God revealed himself to Moses as the omnipotent, unchangeable Sovereign by saying: "I am that I am." He then proceeded to inform Moses that he is the God of Abraham, Isaac, and Jacob, that he promised to deliver Israel, and that Moses should give them the promises of God.

In a vital way, this is what Christians do today in sharing their faith, ministering to needs, and standing for righteousness in society. We reveal the nature of God as revealed to us in the Word of God and convey the promises of God to spiritually lost men. With the Holy Spirit as our personal instructor and the Word of God in an easily understood version, any Christian can serve Christ before mastering the Bible. One need not be a Bible school or seminary graduate to introduce a person to Jesus Christ. Any true believer who knows John 3:16 and companion verses can do that. It is not a question of how much we know, but how much we care. Someone has said, "The key to success in the Christian life is not ability but availability."

3. *No one will believe me!* "Moses answered and said, But, behold, they will not believe me, nor hearken unto my voice" (Exodus 4:1). Fear of rejection is part of the inferiority complex of the melancholy temperament. Moses clearly reveals this fear in his excuse, and he does so in direct contradiction to God's promise. In chapter 3, verse 18, God had promised, "And they shall hearken to thy voice. . . ." What could

be more explicit! God had assured Moses that the people of Israel would believe him, but Moses chose to remember his rejection forty years earlier by some Israelites he tried to help (Exodus 2:11-15). Naturally, he felt he would be repulsed again.

Failure is often devastating to Melancholies. From that point on, their feelings of inferiority increase and they dread to attempt anything lest they repeat their disastrous performance. Right here Mr. Melancholy should take a good look at a very natural habit, that of thinking more of himself than the cause of Christ and the needs of others. One of the best escapes from this mental prison is to focus attention on the ripe harvest field of the world that Jesus said is waiting for spiritual laborers.

Doubtless the judgment seat of Christ will reveal a grievous number of Christians who quenched the Holy Spirit's leading to share their faith because "they will not believe me." This fear is completely selfish! The sooner we recognize and confess it as a sin, the sooner we will experience the power of the Holy Spirit in our lives. We are not responsible for the success or failure of our witness; we are responsible only to give that witness.

4. *I can't speak in public!* Moses' fourth excuse is used by Christians repeatedly. In Moses' words, "I am not eloquent . . . but I am slow of speech, and of a slow tongue." Every pastor and Sunday school teacher has heard this excuse in one form or another. God's answer to Moses is as pertinent today as it was then. "And the Lord said unto him, Who hath made man's mouth? Or who maketh the dumb, or deaf, or the seeing, or the blind? Have not I the Lord? Now therefore go, and I will be with thy mouth and teach thee what thou shalt say" (Exodus 4:11, 12). The question, God said, is not what you can do but what I can do. As is often the case, gifted, scholarly people are not loquacious, but neither are they guilty of saying meaningless things. Though Melancholies may not be dynamic and charismatic like Sanguines, the Holy Spirit certainly can make them effective speakers.

Moses' lame excuse not only slighted the power of God, it saddled him with an assistant, his brother Aaron, who often was a hindrance rather than a help. Moses was not a gifted speaker, but a call to preach or teach the Word of God is not concerned with eloquence — it asks obedience. The Lord's answer to Moses reveals unequivocally that the power of God, not our talents and potential, gains spiritual success. The Christian Melancholy, like Moses, can prove the power of the living God by trusting his direction rather than his own feelings of inadequacy.

As pastor of a church with an active youth ministry, I have gone out of my way to encourage melancholic young men to consider the gospel ministry. We don't need more ministers of melancholy temperament than others, but melancholy youths are prone to think they are unqualified for preaching because they are more inhibited than their sanguine and choleric friends. Such young men need encouragement that speaking competence can be acquired. As sanguine and choleric students have to discipline themselves to learn *what* to say, the Melancholy requires training in learning *how* to say it. By nature, he will set a high standard for study and will strive for superior sermons.

An older minister who had a profound influence on my life surprised me by revealing that as a lad he resisted God's call to preach the gospel because he stuttered severely. He went to college finally with faith that God would remove his impediment. When I met him years later and heard him preach repeatedly, not once did I detect a speech impediment. It would never have been known if he had not mentioned it. Man's inabilities are no measure of God's provision.

5. *I don't want to go.* The irresolute, impractical tendency of a Melancholy is revealed in the last excuse of Moses that incurred the anger of the Lord. "And he said, O my Lord, send, I pray thee, by the hand of him whom thou wilt send" (4:13) — in other words, "I'd appreciate it if you sent someone else." This bares Moses' real reason for not accepting the leadership of Israel — he just didn't want to do it. Melancholy people

have a tendency to clutch preconceived prejudices in the face of contrary facts. Once they make up their minds they can't do something, even good reasoning will not change their minds. God had performed miracles for Moses, had answered every one of his doubts, and had even given him the power to perform miracles, but Moses asked God to send someone else because he didn't want to go. He was on the verge of turning down the greatest opportunity he would ever receive. Only God's insistence and the provision of an assistant persuaded Moses to be available.

It is possible that the fifth excuse of Moses reveals his pent-up hostility and bitterness from forty years of isolation in the wilderness. Humanly speaking, we can understand that when he was willing to give up the pleasures and prestige of Egyptian leadership for his people, only to be rejected by them, he would develop deep resentment. I am inclined to believe this is one of the underlying factors in his rejection of God's call. Sensitive, melancholy people brood and indulge in persecution complexes to their own detriment. Moses' inability to make a common sense decision in the very presence of God was probably caused by a faulty thinking pattern that had persisted for forty years. This poisons the emotional well-being of any temperament, but particularly of a Melancholy. Such feelings are sin and have no place in the heart of a believer. They must be confessed and replaced with thanksgiving by faith in order to maintain fellowship with God (1 Thessalonians 5:18).

Good mental and spiritual hygiene for every temperament, particularly the melancholy, is to refuse to coddle negative and critical thoughts. Since the Melancholy by temperament is a perfectionist, he severely criticizes those who disagree with him. No one can breed bitterness or nurse a grudge like a Melancholy. Such thanklessness not only grieves the Holy Spirit, it produces a very unpleasant personality.

The bitterness of Moses points up the power of forgiveness. I have known many people who were so filled with hatred that they could not think rationally, and some people have unconsciously turned their hatred for one person toward people they really loved. One of the leading causes of sexual impotence in biologically normal men is hatred. It may be subconscious aversion to a domineering, critical mother or a woman who spurned their love, but it can deaden the normal mating drive with a wife they truly love. I have known men that were immediately healed when they got down on their knees and confessed their hatred and asked God to give them a forgiving heart. Forgiveness removed a spiritual cancer.

The remedy for negative, stultifying thinking is not difficult for a Christian. He simply acknowledges bitter thoughts, hostile feelings, and "evil imaginations" about others as sin and confesses them, then he will be released from their power and forgiven by God. A new thinking pattern is built by concentrating on good things and God's good purpose for all. We should not be discouraged if this change does not come immediately, for a pattern is made up of many pieces. An excellent verse of Scripture to memorize and follow is Philippians 4:8: "Finally, brethren, whatever things are true, whatever things are honest, whatever things are just, whatever things are pure, whatever things are lovely, whatever things are of good report; if there be any virtue, and if there be any praise, think on these things."

The excuses of Moses the Melancholy that reveal his inferiority complex are all based on lies. Although they seemed reasonable to him, none was valid — nor helpful. Such feelings limit the effectiveness of any individual. If you are ruled by an inferiority complex, you are limiting God through unbelief. One of your great needs, therefore, is faith, and faith comes through the Word of God, by the Holy Spirit. It is a gift for your taking, and it increases "from faith unto faith" as we obey God's leading step by step to his destination for us.

Moses' anger

In addition to fear, repressed anger often stalks the temperament of a Melancholy. Moses' propensity for anger seared several episodes of his life. His failure to gain control over this emotion cost him the satisfaction of leading his people into the Promised Land. This deep-running anger, which not only grieves the Spirit of God, but sometimes destroys one's health, is fertile soil for irritability.

As you read through Scripture, note such reports as "Moses was angry with them" (Exodus 16:20) and "Moses' anger burned" (Exodus 32:19). Not all anger is wrong, but self-indulgent anger displeases God and leads to serious overt sins.

Moses' anger flared surprisingly after he had experienced many days in the presence of God on the mountain where God wrote the Ten Commandments and gave him Israel's laws. When Moses rejoined the people and saw them indulging in pagan, immoral revelings, he was so angry that he "cast the tables out of his hands, and broke them" (Exodus 32:19). This may have been righteous anger toward evil, but Moses' propensity for wrath produced sin when not controlled.

Anger-motivated actions usually cause problems and intensify difficulties. James 1:20 tells us, "the wrath of man worketh not the righteousness of God." Anger must lead to righteous action for God to be served.

We can appreciate the enormous emotional pressure on Moses in the wilderness. The hot, hungry, disgruntled Israelites took out their frustrations on Moses, complaining bitterly against him whenever they were dissatisfied with God's provisions for them. Few men have faced the pressures he did for such a long period of time. No understanding person would criticize Moses for becoming vexed at these ungrateful people, but the all-sufficient God did. God had offered Moses all the guidance and power he needed, and Moses' neglect of it resulted in sinful self-assertion that marred his testimony and invoked God's judgment.

Toward the end of their exile in the wilderness, when Moses' irritability was at an all-time high, the people besieged him with complaints. Numbers 20:3-5 records their savage verbal assault: "Would God that we had died when our brethren died before the Lord! And why have ye brought up the congregation of the Lord into this wilderness, that we and our cattle should die there? And wherefore have ye made us to come up out of Egypt, to bring us in unto this evil place? It is no place of seed, or of figs, or of vines, or of pomegranates; neither is there any water to drink."

Moses' initial reaction is portrayed in the next verses. "And Moses and Aaron went from the presence of the assembly unto the door of the tabernacle of the congregation, and they fell upon their faces; and the glory of the Lord appeared unto them. And the Lord spoke unto Moses, saying, Take the rod, and gather thou the assembly together . . . and speak ye unto the rock before their eyes; and it shall give forth its water, and thou shalt bring forth to them water out of the rock: so thou shalt give the congregation and their beasts drink."

Then the melancholy nature of Moses erupted in anger. "And Moses took the rod from before the Lord, as he commanded him. And Moses and Aaron gathered the congregation together before the rock, and he said unto them, Hear now, ye rebels; must we fetch you water out of this rock? And Moses lifted up his hand, and with his rod he smote the rock twice; and the water came out abundantly, and the congregation drank, and their beasts also. And the Lord spoke unto Moses and Aaron, Because ye believed me not, to sanctify me in the eyes of the children of Israel, therefore ye shall not bring this congregation into the land which I have given them" (Numbers 20:9-12).

Though Moses' vehemence may seem insignificant, he flagrantly disobeyed the express command of God to *speak* to the rock. God's plan was to show his gracious provision in response to the people's needs, but Moses' impetuous action ruined all that! With an imperious denunciation of the people, he struck the rock twice and the water gushed out. Instead of conveying God's grace and power, Moses communicated his own rage and self-righteousness. His poor example shortened his life and his leadership as God decreed he could not enter the Promised Land. He was given a mountaintop view of the land just prior to his death, but a new, unsullied leader took his place at the front of Israel's army.

Unconfessed anger still causes many heartaches in the lives of God's people. It grieves and suppresses the Spirit, cheats Christians of eternal rewards, and even shortens lives (1 Corinthians 11:30-32). I know a missionary of melancholy temperament who died many years before his time because he refused to admit that his anger was sin. He blamed everyone around him, stewed in his own misery, and died from an overdose of black bile before he reached the normal halfway mark in life! It isn't worth it! We may profit from Moses' experience and enjoy the maximum blessings of God in this life and the life to come by seeking the transforming grace of the Holy Spirit for all forms of angry hostility.

Moses' depression

Moses is one of three great servants of God who became so depressed that he despaired of life and asked God to let him die. The others were Elijah (1 Kings 19) and Jonah (Jonah 4:1-3). Of all the temperaments, melancholy people have the greatest problem with depression. Some very impressive excuses are given to justify depression, but, as I pointed out in the chapter on the subject in *Spirit-Controlled Temperament,* depression is the emotional result of *self-pity.* It doesn't matter what temperament you are, if you indulge in self-pity you will be depressed. Melancholy people experience more depression because they tend to indulge in self-pity more than others. They can be gracious and kind outwardly but be suffering in self-pity which if indulged long enough, will develop into a persecution complex or apathetic state.

The account of Moses' depression is given in Numbers 11: 10-15 for our admonition and profit. In the account we find Moses' angry thinking pattern going from bad to worse. Instead of looking to God for his needs when the people complained about the heaven-sent bread called manna, he began to feel sorry for himself. "Wherefore hast thou afflicted thy servant . . . that thou layest the burden of all this people upon me?" Moses moaned. How human; and how wrong! God never asked Moses to bear all this burden or responsibility; it was God's! Moses cultivated so much pity for himself that he asked God: "Kill me, I pray thee, out of hand."

Have you ever felt so burdened that you wanted to die? If so, I suggest that it wasn't the size of your burdens that crushed you, but your attitude toward them. Attitude forms your thinking patterns which produce your feelings. If your attitude is consistently thankful to God, you cannot become depressed. But if you focus on unfavorable circumstances around you, you will frequently be depressed. Remember, Moses' reaction to the situation caused his depression, not the circumstances in themselves. God promises to sustain us at all times, and since he cannot fail it is our refusal to believe him and appropriate his supply that produces self-pity and depression.

One reassuring aspect of this story is that God disregarded Moses' request to die. Evidently the melancholy servant confessed his sin of self-pity, for God went on to use him for many years. This should bring hope to depressed saints who, like Moses, have prayed for death. God forgives us and uses our lives. He did the same to Elijah and Jonah. If, however, you are in severe depression, you face a decision. Will you give thanks no matter what the outlook, as commanded by God, or will you go right on indulging your self-pity? You decide whether or not you will be healed, and Christ waits to heal you.

Moses' perfectionism

As a Melancholy, Moses was a perfectionist. In spite of those moments of carnality mentioned above, Moses' talents were yielded to God. If you read the latter half of Exodus and the books of Numbers and Leviticus, you will see how God used this characteristic. God gave Moses the meticulously minute details of his law: the ceremonial law, the governmental law, and the instruction of the priesthood. He also gave Moses the specific measurements and materials for building the tabernacle, the Israelites' center of worship for hundreds of years.

God's standard of righteousness is so exact that only a Spirit-filled Melancholy like Moses could have been his instrument for such an undertaking. One of the outstanding instruments of blessing to the people of God in Old Testament days was the tabernacle, provided by the grace of God through the perfectionist traits of Moses which were yielded to the Holy Spirit. God is ever seeking such traits to bless the lives of men.

Probably as a product of this perfectionist ability, Melancholies have a difficult time delegating authority and responsibility. A prime illustration of that in Moses' life is found in the 18th chapter of Exodus. His father-in-law, Jethro, who came to visit Moses and his daughter, found his son-in-law so busy administering laws that he couldn't spend any time with his family. Moses was so conscientious that he was trying to help everyone who wanted to come to him. Working from morning to night, he returned home exhausted. Jethro counseled: "The thing that thou doest is not good. Thou wilt surely wear away, both thou, and this people that are with thee; for this thing is too heavy for thee; thou art not able to perform it thyself alone" (18:17, 18). He then advised Moses to select qualified men to divide the populace into small groups and rule over their affairs. Moses heeded this advice and helped everyone!

This story is used in business management courses as an illustration of how to cure an organizational problem. Much of the creative genius of a melancholy person is lost because he is reluctant to assign to others the work that needs to be accomplished. As a rule, he has an innate distrust for the abilities of others, and thus tends to do everything himself. D. L. Moody used to advise: "Instead of doing the work of ten men, get ten men to work." When motivated by the Holy Spirit, Mr. Melancholy will tend to get his eyes off details and onto important projects. As the vision of a lost world burns into his heart and mind, he will tend to put a premium on motivating others instead of being a one-man band. He may have to settle for work beneath his standard of perfection, but the net result will be far greater productivity in the cause of Christ.

Moses' reorganization program freed him from details, thus reserving his time for things of major importance.

Some men will admit, "But I like to do these things myself." Although they do a terrific job by themselves, it is only a fraction of what they could accomplish had they trusted God and other people. I know a man who does the work of three people, but if he were not afraid of rejection and didn't have a low esteem of others' capabilities, he could delegate authority and accomplish the work of ten. When this is pointed out to him, he gets defensive and protests, "But we can't find adequate help," or, "I'm afraid other people will do it wrong and I'll have to do it over anyway." By contrast, the Spirit-filled Melancholy will think big. Most people by nature have too little vision, and this is particularly a weakness of Mr. Melancholy.

Moses' loyalty

One of the most admirable traits of a Melancholy is his loyalty and faithfulness. Although he does not make friends easily he is intensely loyal to those he acquires. This characteristic makes him particularly devoted to God when filled with the Spirit. When Moses turned his life over to God, he became an example of this dedication, directed by the Holy Spirit. He was so transformed that he changed from an insecure, doubtful, pessimistic, compulsive, depressed man to the responsible father-image for the people, who responded to his leadership. As Moses walked with God, so the Israelites walked.

Moses' devotion seems to have grown through the forty years he served God. As problems arose, he turned to God for guidance. When the people complained of hunger, Moses prayed and God answered with manna from heaven (Exodus 16). When they needed water, he struck the rock and God supplied an abundance of water (Exodus 17). When they needed the waters of the Red Sea rolled back, he struck them with his rod in the name of the Lord and God miraculously separated the waters (Exodus 14). The man's faith is a tribute to what God can do with a fearful, negative, melancholy temperament dedicated to his will.

The information is so complete concerning the life and ministry of Moses that the reader would be wise to study Exodus 1—20; 24:9-18; 32—34; and the book of Numbers. The transforming power of the Holy Spirit is demonstrated on almost every page. This does not mean that Moses was perfect. You will come upon several failures in his life that indicate he was very human during the years he served God. That, of course, is what makes the Bible such a believable book: it portrays both the successes and failures of its heroes because, as they say today, "That's the way it is." God doesn't use perfect men — there aren't any. He uses men who trust him. Every successful servant of God has had to get up off the canvas of failure at some time in his life, confess his unbelief, and ask God to use him again.

Even the greatest of Spirit-filled Christians have proved their humanity by failure. Almost every great saint I know admits to apologizing to some brother for something said or done. Moses is a good example of Spirit-filled temperament, not because he was perfect, but because most of the time he was pliable in the hand of God. Melancholy Christians' failure to be perfect often digs another pitfall: "If I can't be perfect, I won't try at all." And they quit. To Moses' credit, although he fell many times, each time he confessed his sin, re-yielding his life to God, and went on as a transformed Melancholy. God wants to do the same in every life. Right now, instead of fretting over your weaknesses, thank God for his power in your life and trust him to transform you.

7

ABRAHAM THE PHLEGMATIC

The easiest people to get along with in life are Phlegmatics. Their calm, easygoing nature makes them well liked by others, and their clever wit and dry humor makes them a joy to have around. They qualify for the "Mr. Nice Guy" label wherever they go. In fact, Phlegmatics are usually such good people that they act more like Christians before their salvation than other temperament types afterward.

Mr. Phlegmatic, in addition to being calm and easygoing, is a cheerful fellow who works well with others. He is an efficient, conservative, dependable, witty person with a practical turn of mind. Since he is quite introvertish, as a rule, his weaknesses, like his strengths, are not as readily perceptible as those of the more expressive temperaments. But he does have some, the greatest of which is lack of motivation. He can ignore work graciously and is prone to be stubborn, stingy, and indecisive. He has an ability to look at life through the eyes of a spectator and seek to avoid "getting involved" with anything. Phlegmatics make good diplomats since they are natural peacemakers. Many are teachers, doctors, scientists, comedians, and magazine and book editors. When externally motivated they make very capable leaders.

As a professional observer of people, I have concluded that when filled with the Spirit, and thus properly motivated, Phlegmatics make unusually successful servants of Christ. They never volunteer to serve as leaders, but they have latent leadership capabilities and, because of their efficient, gracious way with others, do not seem to create friction.

Several years ago I elected to have a professionally trained school teacher lead our vacation Bible school program during the summer. She was predominantly choleric in temperament and tackled the job with characteristic intensity. We enjoyed a very good school that year, exceptionally efficient and well run. However, she tended to be sharp and abrasive with people. In fact, the next year we experienced a very difficult time securing workers. About that time I was in the midst of my first serious studies of temperament. As a result, I developed a growing respect for the phlegmatic temperament as a source of untapped help. Rather than give up my idea of having a professionally trained educator run our VBS program, I urged the Christian education board to seek a Phlegmatic to take the job. Naturally she was reluctant — Phlegmatics usually are — but we persisted. Finally she agreed, and we have been delighted with the results. Not only have we enjoyed a well-planned and efficient school, but a director who is so easy to work with that we have little trouble getting others to participate when they discover that Mrs. Phlegmatic is the superintendent.

One important thing to keep in mind when trying to motivate a Phlegmatic — don't take no for an answer. At the same time, don't be obnoxiously forceful or he will stiffen his back and stubbornly, though graciously, resist your most aggressive entreaties. Present your case and expect to be refused — the first time around. Gently leave the door open and draw. back, allowing him sufficient breathing room to think calmly and to pray about it. Occasionally approach him, but don't press him for a quick decision. Give him plenty of encouragement and be as factual as you can. You can't trick or "psych" him, but if you appeal to his sense of Christian responsibility, he will gradually respond.

For years I disdained enlisting Phlegmatics because they

did not seem to respond to my enthusiasm. I erroneously interpreted this as disinterest. In actuality, they just don't get enthusiastic about much of anything, but that is *not* the measure of their capability.

Looking back over the last five years since I have consistently tried to employ Phlegmatics in the work of the Lord, I must say I am very pleased with the results. Although it took a little longer to get them committed, most of them are still consistently turning out effective work. The Sanguines have enthusiastically rushed in but, like whipping cream, have been inclined to melt under the heat of routine service. The Cholerics have volunteered their services and done a good job, but we have treated some emotionally scarred victims of their caustic tongues all over the church. Melancholies who could be persuaded to think of others long enough to accept a place of service have often been short termers also. They are critical of the way we do things because we don't measure up to their standards or they are offended by the hustle and bustle of Sunday school or youth hijinks and ride the first black mood back out of circulation.

Not so the Phlegmatics! Week after week they are in their place in the department or youth group, quietly organizing and efficiently serving with good humor. That is, if you can get them motivated at the outset. Oh, yes, there are outstanding exceptions to this negative catalog of temperament failures. These are the Spirit-controlled Sanguines, Cholerics, Melancholies, and Phlegmatics. As the Spirit of God transforms them, they show a consistency and fruitfulness foreign to their temperament. That is what makes working with Christians in the local church such an exciting and rewarding experience.

For the benefit of the Phlegmatics who read this section, I would like to offer a special suggestion. So far, I have yet to find a Phlegmatic who has taken on more than he can accomplish. Since it is your natural inclination to be overprotective of yourself, pray earnestly about an opportunity before you decide to turn it down. Examine your excuses for non-involvement to see if it is the Holy Spirit's leading or your own selfishness. Telling yourself, "There are so many others who can do a better job than I," can be a form of selfishness. Since most Phlegmatics have a fear of failure before others, they are reluctant to launch out on seas of service where others can watch them sink. Forget that selfish thinking pattern! Ask God for his leading, and if he gives you a burden for that work, take the responsibility and trust him to supply the ability to do the job. Philippians 4:13 says you can do it. Since most Phlegmatics tend to underestimate their abilities, you should memorize that verse and learn to trust God's power instead of your phlegmatic fears. You will be thrilled at what God can do with a Phlegmatic who is fully yielded to his will.

"Likewise reckon ye also yourselves to be dead indeed unto sin, but alive unto God through Jesus Christ our Lord. Let not sin therefore reign in your mortal body, that ye should obey it in the lusts thereof. Neither yield ye your members as instruments of unrighteousness unto sin, but yield yourselves unto God, as those that are alive from the dead, and your members as instruments of righteousness unto God" (Romans 6: 11-13).

The lack of motivation so characteristic of the phlegmatic temperament is discussed with clever satire by Alexander Whyte in his notes on the temperaments. We include his lengthy quotation here for your interest.

"Sloth sums up, in one short and expressive word, the bad side of this temperament. Some part of what we call sloth in some men is, no doubt, in fairness to be set down to such a Phlegmatic constitution that it would take the will and the energy of a giant to overcome it. There are men of such a slow-working heart, their blood creeps through their veins at such a snail's pace, their joints are so loosely knit, and their whole body is so lethargic, that both God and man must take all into consideration before they condemn them. And when we must say sloth in his case, we still take into account all that can be said in extenuation, and the Phlegmatic man will not be blamed for what he could not help. He will be blamed and chastised only for what he could quite well have helped if only he had resolved to help it. At the same time, sloth is sloth, laziness is laziness, whatever your temperament may be. Laziness, indeed, is not of the body at all; it is of the mind. It is not their temperaments that make shipwrecks of so many of our students' and of our ministers' lives.

"The Phlegmatic minister has not worked harder on Sabbath than some of his people have worked every day of all the week. But he is a minister, and he has no master beside him but his own conscience, and so he spends all Monday on the sofa with a newspaper and a novel. He will read for his pulpit tomorrow forenoon, and visit his sick in the afternoon. But tomorrow he is not very well in the morning, and it rains in the afternoon. On Wednesday he still has four whole days before Sabbath, and besides, his letters are in terrible arrears; he has not had time to answer a note for a fortnight. A friend drops in to spend Thursday with him, but what of that? He has all Friday and Saturday to be kept shut up and absolutely sacred. On Friday afternoon he is told that his old elder, who was so ill, is dead, and he is as unhappy a man all that day as you could wish him to be. And he has a very unhappy errand before him that afternoon in having to explain to the bereaved family how busy he was all the beginning of the week. He sits into Saturday morning seeking for his Sabbath text, but has to go to bed before he has found it. All Saturday he has his meals at his desk, and he is like a bear robbed of her whelps if anybody but looks at him or speaks to him. On Sabbath morning he takes an old rag out of his drawer, and his people look at one another, as he cannot even read it. Brother minister, of the most remote and illiterate congregation in Scotland, sit down to thy desk early every day, and if God has made thee of a slothful, lethargic, phlegmatic temperament, only sit down to thy desk doggedly. Let every lazy student of divinity, and with him every waiting, complaining, postponing probationer, go drown himself at once."

Actually, there is a better solution to the phlegmatic temperament's natural sloth or lack of motivation than drowning.

One of the nine strengths of the Holy Spirit (Galatians 5:22-23) is "self-control." Therefore the filling of the Holy Spirit will keep the Phlegmatic from indulging the flesh and will motivate him to service. As he feeds on the Word and yields his mind to the Holy Spirit, he will be given goals and plans that motivate him. The secret of motivation is not high blood pressure, enthusiasm, or energy. It is vision! Whenever a person has goals and objectives he is motivated. Consequently, the Spirit-filled Phlegmatic will be a motivated person and his daily life will be a demonstration of transformed temperament. Phlegmatics concerned about a greater motivation to glorify God should study the goal-setting techniques of the Apostle Paul described in Chapter 5.

Several of the men God used in Bible days seem to possess a high degree of phlegmatic temperament: Noah, Samuel, Daniel, Joseph (the husband of Mary), Nathaniel, Philip, and the Apostle James. The best illustration for the purposes of our study is Abraham. Revered by more people than any man except the Lord Jesus, Abraham would never have achieved greatness without the transforming power of the Holy Spirit. His lifetime struggles with a phlegmatic temperament provide us with an ideal illustration of what God can do with a phlegmatic yielded to his will and filled with his Spirit. When he walked in the Spirit, depending on the Lord, he was highly successful. But when he grieved the Spirit through fear and doubt he was a total failure. It is the same with us today. Hopefully, we will profit by the experiences of Abraham the Phlegmatic.

Cautious

The natural hesitancy, indecision, and fear of a Phlegmatic are seen in Abraham the first time he appears in the Bible. He was a resident of Ur of the Chaldees, shortly after the days of Nimrod and the destruction of the tower of Babel. Archeological research indicates that Ur was a highly developed city, comparable to Babylon in the days of Nebuchadnezzar 1,000 years later. It also was heavily influenced by the idolatrous religion of Babylon begun by Nimrod and his mother Semiramis.

This evil city located in "the cradle of civilization" was no place for the young man and his wife whom God had selected to be the ancestors of his chosen people. For that reason God called Abram (as he was known then) out of that country, saying, "Get thee out of thy country, and from thy kindred, and from thy father's house, unto a land that I will show thee" (Genesis 12:1). But Abram was so dependent on his father and relatives that instead of going all the way with God, he stopped in Haran with his family. Not until his father Terah died and God spoke to him again did Abraham obey, and even then he took his nephew Lot with him.

It seems to be very difficult for Phlegmatics to trust God fully. This is probably because fear is one of their most common problems. Their tendency to be anxious for everything and to become professional worriers is not as severe as for those of the melancholy temperament, but it does tend to limit them. Many Christian Phlegmatics are reluctant to enter the door of opportunity when it opens. It is not lack of capability that keeps Phlegmatics from the upper echelon of success, but reluctance to venture out onto the uncharted seas of the unknown. Quite characteristic is Abram's reluctance to leave his father, and then he took along his nephew Lot as a sort of "security blanket" to this unknown land God had promised him. The Phlegmatic becomes dynamically usable in the hands of God only when he learns to trust God alone. His security blanket usually turns out to cause an unnecessary problem in his life, as Lot was to Abraham.

The promises of God as given to Abraham in Genesis 12:1-3 are in the past tense, indicating that God had already made these promises to him and is now reiterating them. It took several years for Phlegmatic Abraham to learn to trust in God. God extended six promises to him: (1) "I will make of thee a great nation," (2) "I will bless thee," (3) "I will make thy name great," (4) "Thou shalt be a blessing," (5) "I will bless them that bless thee and curse him that curseth thee," (6) "In thee shall all families of the earth be blessed."

If Abraham had taken God at his word, he would have experienced much less heartache and confusion. Faith is simply taking God at his word and launching out upon his promises. God has never proven unfaithful to anyone, but every generation of Christians, particularly those of the phlegmatic temperament, have to learn Abraham's lessons all over again. Later God spoke to Abraham and gave him another promise which specifically said, "Unto thy seed will I give this land" (12: 7). Abraham was seventy-five years of age, so fathering children was unlikely but still humanly possible; therefore, God chose to let time elapse until it became biologically impossible, and then he miraculously fulfilled his promise as an illustration of his faithfulness, not only to Abraham but to Christians of all generations.

The Bible teaches us that God increases our faith by testing. James 1:2-4 states, "My brethren, count it all joy when ye fall into various trials, knowing this, that the testing of your faith worketh patience. But let patience have her perfect work, that ye may be perfect and entire, lacking nothing." This principle of God operated in the life of Abraham, and it teaches us that we should expect our faith to be tested, and instead of grumbling or seeking a human solution, we should thank God for the testing and trust him for the solution. This formula always succeeds.

Shortly after God gave his promises to Abram, he tested the pioneer. Genesis 12:10 states, "And there was a famine in the land; and Abram went down into Egypt to sojourn there, for the famine was grievous in the land." Egypt, like Lot, was a false security blanket for Abram. Having come from a center of civilization to a wilderness area seared by famine, Abram looked to the nearest proven area of supply, the land of Egypt. Without consulting God for direction, he took his family into that pagan land, similar to the one from which God had called him. His disgraceful failure in Egypt, which we will examine later, would never have occurred had he waited for his deliverance, which would have come in the land of Canaan. All fear-prone Christians should claim the promise, "Faithful is he that calleth you, who also will do it" (1 Thessalonians 5:24).

Peaceable

One of the most admirable characteristics of Phlegmatics is their love for peace. They tend to exhibit a serenity and calmness that is soothing to others. Usually their desire for peace and harmony is greater than their desire for personal possessions, a trait revealed in Abraham when his herdsmen and the herdsmen of Lot began to strive with each other. Since both were heads of families and had servants, they kept their flocks and herds separated. But without fences, it was natural that conflict arose over grazing land and water sources. Abram offered a solution by saying to Lot: "Let there be no strife, I pray thee, between me and thee, and between my herdsmen and thy herdsmen; for we are brethren. Is not the whole land before thee? Separate thyself, I pray thee, from me; if thou wilt take the left hand, then I will go to the right; or if thou depart to the right hand, then I will go to the left" (13:8, 9). This seems a pleasant solution for a trying situation. But it is likely that Abram suffered much heartache by separating himself from his human security blanket. That Lot proved unworthy of such reliance did not lessen Abram's pain.

It seems no coincidence that "after that Lot was separated from him" God gave Abram the specific title deed for the land of Canaan. God wants to bless his children, but he requires absolute faith, for "without faith it is impossible to please him" (Hebrews 11:6).

If we are unwilling to trust the Lord completely, we lose blessings he has in store for us or he permits trials to come our way to bring us to rely upon him. If Abram and Lot had not separated, it seems that God could not have promised the following blessing: "Lift up now thine eyes, and look from the place where thou art northward, and southward, and eastward, and westward: For all the land which thou seest, to thee will I give it, and to thy seed forever. And I will make thy seed as the dust of the earth: so that if a man can number the dust of the earth, then shall thy seed also be numbered. Arise, walk through the land in the length of it and in the breadth of it; for I will give it unto thee" (Genesis 13:14-17).

Many a Christian worker has come to the place where he must separate himself from loved ones and friends in order to enter the appointed place of God's blessing. Practically every missionary and most ministers of the gospel have faced that traumatic decision; and many laymen must likewise face it, for God has a particular plan for all of his children. Many a young person has chosen to attend a college that was convenient rather than a Christian school that required extra cost or sacrifice. Most pastors can produce a list of "shipwrecked" young people whose faith foundered on a secular campus. This is not to imply that God wants all Christian young people to attend a Christian college. But most pastors and counselors believe God has led far more to Christian colleges than have gone, and the failure is usually unbelief on the part of the parents or the student.

One of the hardest decisions I ever made was to send my eighteen-year-old daughter 2,500 miles away from home to a Christian college. I well remember thinking at the time that it was like cutting one-fourth of my heart out of my body and sending it far from me. Only two years later another fourth of my heart had to be cut away when my son made the same decision. No doubt the day will come when the two younger children will face the same decision. In retrospect, I have no misgivings. It cost us the enjoyment of their presence and many happy hours and days of fellowship, but it has been well worth it. Both young people are walking with God and preparing to serve him, which has more than compensated for the "heart surgery" this loving father experienced. Their mother and I thank God regularly that we did not limit his use of their lives by clinging to them, but abandoned them to his perfect will.

Reliable

"What you are under pressure is what you are!" is one of my longstanding convictions. Pressure does not change our character — it just identifies its true nature. Of all the temperament types, Mr. Phlegmatic by nature comes out best under pressure. Sanguines often run off half-cocked in the wrong direction, and Melancholies may go to pieces under pressure, but Cholerics and Phlegmatics both rise to occasions of difficulty. The Choleric tends to rely on intuitive judgment in such emergencies and many times lacks the organization and efficiency that is a hallmark of the Phlegmatic. One of the behavioral surprises in a study of human nature is the calm, efficient reaction of the Phlegmatic in a time of great crisis. The fourteenth chapter of Genesis recounts such an experience in the life of Abraham.

Shortly after Lot became a resident of Sodom, war broke out among the kings of Canaan. Chedorlaomer, king of Elam, and several other kings conquered Sodom and Gomorrah and took many inhabitants as slaves, including Lot and his family. One of the captives escaped and revealed the disaster to Abram. The Bible describes Abram's reaction in these words: "And when Abram heard that his brother was taken captive, he armed his trained servants, born in his own house, three hundred and eighteen, and pursued them unto Dan. And he divided himself against them, he and his servants, by night, and smote them, and pursued them unto Hobah, which is on the left hand of Damascus. And he brought back all the goods, and also brought again his brother Lot, and his goods, and the women also, and the people" (14:14-16).

This exciting story reveals several things about Phlegmatic Abraham and others of his temperament. Their concern for loved ones in an emergency takes precedence over their love for personal safety and emotional protection. When motivated to action and committed to the battle, Phlegmatic Abraham revealed latent leadership characteristics that were extremely effective. His method of attacking an army of superior forces is a model that has been used many times since in the annals of warfare. By dividing his small band and using the cover of darkness and the element of surprise, he not only overcame a superior army but relentlessly pursued them until he was victorious. His calm, unemotional response to victory is also characteristic of the Phlegmatic. We do not find a single illustration of braggadocio in the life of Abraham. This is not only a tribute to his spiritual life, but a distinctive of Phlegmatics in general, who are prone to be conservative about everything, including self-praise. Abraham knew — as Melchizedek, the priest of Salem, later pointed out — that victory was really due to the blessing of God, who delivered him from his enemy. For that reason he faithfully gave tithes of all he possessed to God through the priest.

If the truth were known and the financial records of evangelical churches could some day be computed, I am confident that Phlegmatics would be accounted the most consistent in the practice of tithing. Doubtless they are not the ones who talk about it most, but when once committed to a principle of God, they are prone to be the most regular. Sanguines are ever making new vows of faithfulness whereas Cholerics are usually so overcommitted financially they keep putting off gifts to the Lord, which is tantamount to not doing it at all. Melancholies are likely to be fearful that they cannot live on the rest of their income and so are reluctant to commit themselves to tithing. Phlegmatics, more than any other temperament, are inclined to do the "acceptable thing." They are the most prone of all the temperaments to obey what God expects of a Christian. However, once having committed themselves to tithing, their somewhat thrifty nature makes them least spontaneous in giving offerings. The other temperaments would be more susceptible to spontaneously responding to a particular need. Not so the Phlegmatic, who is regular and consistent in his giving habits. When truly transformed by the Holy Spirit, however, his liberated emotions will open his pocketbook.

Passive

The natural tendency of the Phlegmatic to be a peacemaker, as already illustrated, carries with it a tendency to be passive in the face of conflict unless crisis is involved. This often results in male Phlegmatics being "henpecked" by their wives. In the early days of his marriage Abram seemed to be no exception. The sixteenth chapter of Genesis shows Sarai's great influence over her husband. Becoming impatient for God to fulfill his promise of a son to perpetuate their seed, Sarai devised her own plan. Since she was unable to bear him children, she suggested that he take her Egyptian maid named Hagar and "obtain children by her." Abram's agreement produced one of the most regrettable events in the Bible, for it brought into the family of nations a people who would perpetually be in conflict with the promised people of God.

The Bible tells us, "And Abram hearkened to the voice of Sarai." The tragedy of Hagar's pregnancy, her rejection by Sarai, and her ultimate expulsion from the family in order to keep peace is a sad picture of Abram's henpecked state. He loved Ishmael, his son by Hagar, but did not have the strength to resist his wife even after the mistake was made. It would be hard to describe the emotional trauma that must have been Abram's when, after Isaac was born, he sent away Ishmael, whom he loved, to please his wife.

One of the lessons which peace-loving Phlegmatics need to learn is that nothing is ever accomplished by compromise. Peacemaking is admirable if it can be done legitimately, but if it requires compromise of principle it must be paid for in the long run. Many a phlegmatic man, in order to keep peace at home, has allowed his wife to "rule the roost." It is impossible for him to have a spiritual home or develop an effective Christian testimony unless he is the head of his house. Young people who grow up in feminine-dominated homes are emotionally unprepared to face society. Most feminine domination could have been averted if the young husband had assumed the dominant role in his home immediately in obedience to God's will.

I have interviewed Phlegmatics in the counseling room who hated their wives and accordingly had no spiritual vitality whatsoever. Through the years they had acquiesced to their wives' leadership, but resentment had mounted in direct proportion to their own loss of authority. Ultimately this resentment will destroy love because it is unnatural for a woman to dominate a man. Such a situation is not only undesirable for the husband, but will become a source of misery for the wife, who cannot truly respect a mate she does not look up to. Phlegmatic Abraham offers a good example in this respect because the New Testament reveals that God modified his temperament and he became the dominant leader in his home. Ultimately Sarai acknowledged him as her spiritual leader and the family head (1 Peter 3:1-6).

Many a strong-willed woman rebels at the biblical concept of the wife's being in submission to her husband, for by nature she finds it much easier to take over the situation, make the decisions, and boss everyone in the house including her husband. Invariably this withers happiness.

Fearful

It is almost impossible to exaggerate the negative, destructive effects of fear. Hundreds of books have been written on overcoming fear and anxiety. The widespread use of such books and the repeated admonitions of "fear not" in the Word of God mark fear as a universal problem. Of the four temperaments, the one least predisposed to fear is the choleric. Mr. Sanguine, in spite of his false bravado, possesses an underlying insecurity and fear that occasionally bother him. Both Mr. Melancholy and Mr. Phlegmatic have a generous dose of fear, and thus Moses and Abraham had no small problem from innate fears. The only true cure for this temperament predisposition is the supernatural power of God. Moses and Abraham are prime illustrations that this negative aspect of our temperament is transformed when God has control of our lives.

In spite of many of the positive things we have said about

Phlegmatic Abraham, he nevertheless committed two repre-hensible acts of cowardice under the influence of fear.

The first is recorded in the twelfth chapter of Genesis. Be-cause there was famine in the land, Abram forsook God's will and went to Egypt. Knowing that the king of Egypt owned a large harem and did not discriminate, in his selection of wives and concubines, between married and single women, Abram became fearful. As Abram considered Sarai, he real-ized she was very beautiful and he feared the Egyptians might kill him for his beautiful wife. Therefore he suggested, "Say, I pray thee, thou art my sister; that it may be well with me for thy sake; and my soul shall live because of thee." Sure enough, beautiful Sarai was noticed and ushered into the pres-ence of the king. Thinking that Abram was her brother, he treated Abram well for her sake. Only through a plague from God did Pharaoh become aware of the truth and Abram and his wife were spared serious sin. Abram's cowardly fear resulted in his banishment from the country and a very poor witness for God in the pagan nation. This blemish on Abram's life would not have occurred had he trusted God for his food and safety.

Once was not enough for Abram to betray Sarai out of fear. Many years later, as revealed in the twentieth chapter, Abra-ham again asked Sarai to acknowledge him as her brother in an attempt to curry favor with the heathen king Abimelech. Again she was selected for her beauty and was almost added to the king's harem. Had God not warned Abimelech in a dream, Abraham and Sarai would have been involved in a tragic sin. God was prepared to slay Abimelech to prevent the nullification of his promises to Abram and Sarai. God's stan-dards of morality include no exceptions — lying is sin and adultery is sin, even when thought necessary to spare life. Our pretexts and compromises never improve on God's plan and provision.

Unbelief was the greatest problem of Abram, or Abraham, as he was renamed. As he grew in grace and knowledge of the Lord, he was so transformed that this tendency was obliterated from his thinking.

As we look carefully into the story, we find that God cured Abraham's fear by revealing himself in greater measure. The more Abraham learned about God, the more he trusted him — the less fearful he was. The Lord spoke to Abraham in a vision and said, "Fear not, Abram: I am thy shield, and thy exceedingly great reward" (Genesis 15:1). At first Abraham was reluctant to use God as his protector and ultimate rewarder. Instead he looked around for human solutions. Whenever he followed human ingenuity, he stumbled into failure, but when he acted on the promises of God he experienced miracles. Eventually God performed a biological miracle on the bodies of aged Abraham and Sarah so that they became the parents of Isaac and, through him, of the Israelite nation.

Until the birth of Isaac, Abraham's faith was a growing experience, sometimes faltering and then forging ahead. Ultimately he became known as the "father of the faithful," the forebear of those who have put their faith in God.

This does not mean that Abraham invariably obeyed God. It means that his faith became the example of true, unconditional submission to God for all who would know the Savior. God uses a yielded vessel despite lapses when failures are confessed. The key to consistent faith is hearing God's Word, obeying it as the reliable guide of a loving Father, and confessing and forsaking every lapse.

Abraham's transformation

The strength of Abraham's faith is dramatically illustrated in his sacrifice of his son Isaac at God's command. Genesis 22 tells us "God did test Abraham" by instructing him to take the son whom he loved and "offer him for a burnt offering upon the mountains which I will tell thee of." Abraham took his son up Mount Moriah and prepared to sacrifice him. When young Isaac asked about a lamb for the burnt offering, Abraham replied, "My son, God will provide himself a lamb for a burnt offering." Then he bound his son and placed him upon the altar, with knife raised to execute Isaac as God had ordered. But God only wanted Abraham's supreme loyalty, not his son's body. He stopped Abraham and said, "Now I know that thou fearest God, seeing thou hast not withheld . . . thine only son from me." God provided a ram as a substitute offering, for Isaac's death, a picture of the manner in which Jesus Christ many generations later would become the perfect offering for the sins of all mankind. Abraham, the father of the faithful, was asked to be willing to give his son; God actually gave his only begotten Son.

The growth of Abraham's faith illustrates the gradual growth of faith that God provides every believer. We see him transformed from the man in the twelfth chapter who did not have faith enough to trust God for food to the unwavering servant who, as the Holy Spirit reveals in Hebrews 11:19, believed God so implicitly that he expected God to resurrect Isaac if he died on the altar.

Where did Abraham get that faith? By taking God at his word and acting on his promises. God had explicitly promised a posterity to Isaac, and Abraham believed death could not prevent it. Faith does not need answers, but only direction. Many Christians say, "If I knew how this would turn out, I could trust God." This is unbelief. The transformation of Abraham made him one of the greatest men who ever lived, not because he had a phlegmatic temperament but in spite of it. Transformation of temperament is available for every child of God who will be filled with the Spirit and directed by the Word of God.

8

THE TRANSFORMED WALK

The secret of transformed temperament is the filling of the Holy Spirit, not just on a single occasion, but on a continual basis. Much discouragement has assailed believers who erroneously thought that the filling of the Spirit was a once-for-all experience, but Ephesians 5:18 commands us to be continually refilled with the Spirit. A literal translation would read, "And be not drunk with wine, wherein is excess, but be ye being filled with the Spirit." That is, be ye continually in the action of being filled with the Spirit. This parallels the admonition in Galatians 5:16, "This I say then, walk in the Spirit and ye shall not fulfill the lusts of the flesh." Obedience to the flesh is an external indication that we are not internally filled with the Spirit. The cure for this temperament tendency is "walking in the Spirit," which is not the same as being filled with the Spirit. It is dependent on it, but these are not synonymous expressions.

How to be filled with the Spirit

In my book *Spirit-Controlled Temperament* I devoted a chapter to the filling of the Spirit. It would be helpful for the reader to review that chapter in detail. Briefly, the five steps for being filled with the Spirit are as follows:

1. Examine yourself and confess all known sin (1 John 1: 9).
2. Submit yourself completely to God (Romans 6:11-13).
3. Ask to be filled with the Spirit (Luke 11:13).
4. Take God at his word and believe you are filled (Romans 14:23).
5. Thank him for his filling, and repeat this procedure each time you realize you have sinned (1 Thessalonians 5:18).

Occasionally someone protests, "But that is too simple; being filled with the Spirit must be much more complex!" Why must it be difficult? How hard was it for you to obey the Lord's command, "Ye must be born again"? As an eight-year-old boy I became conscious of my need and simply asked the Lord Jesus to come into my heart, cleanse my life, and become my master. He instantly answered my request. Why should he not answer when I ask to be filled with the Holy Spirit? If we have taken steps one and two, then we take step three and we are filled with the Spirit. A. B. Simpson used to say, "Being filled with the Spirit is as easy as breathing; you can simply breathe out and breathe in."

One of the reasons some Christians are reluctant to think they are filled with the Spirit is that they don't see an immediate change in their lives, or the change is of short duration. Two factors have an important bearing on this: temperament and habit, and they work together. The weaknesses of our temperament have created strong habits which involuntarily recur. The instant sin enters, the filling ends and the disappointed Christian concludes: "It doesn't work for me."

For illustration, let us consider a fear-prone melancholy or phlegmatic Christian. These people have a deeply ingrained habit of doubt, negativism, worry, and anxiety. I can predict the thinking pattern of such a person after he follows the five steps of being filled with the Spirit. Before long his negative thinking habit will stir doubts: "Am I filled with the Spirit? I don't feel any different. I'm still afraid." This mental attitude is sin, and the Spirit's filling and control ends.

What such people need to realize is that our feelings are the result of thought patterns. You *feel* negative when you have been *thinking* negatively. A typical illustration may be found in the experience of lust. A college lad who came to me for counseling confessed his "overpowering sex urges." They had become so strong that he was afraid he might try to attack some woman on a dark street. He was primarily concerned about becoming "abnormal" or even a "pervert."

An investigation of his thinking pattern uncovered the following: he habitually viewed Hollywood's wide-screen filth, he regularly read pornographic literature, and he admitted imagining himself in the role of the immoral men he read about. Is it any wonder that he developed strong sexual urges that might lead to something vile and criminal? Since he professed to be a Christian, he confessed his sins of the mind and asked to be filled with the Holy Spirit. At first his inordinate sex desires subsided, but before the day was over he called frantically to report their return. I wasn't surprised. The first good-looking, scantily dressed girl he saw caused him to lust, which grieved the Holy Spirit, and he reverted to his old feelings. He had to understand that his strong sexual feelings would abate only when his mind was renewed by new patterns of wholesome thinking.

You can't fill your mind with filth and expect to feel clean. But this is the reason many Christians "don't see anything wrong" with certain sins. They have been indulging in sinful mental attitudes so long that sinful actions seem normal. I have had people try to justify adultery because they "didn't feel it was wrong." In actuality, they had felt it was wrong before it became commonplace in their thinking pattern. We need to learn that "feelings" cannot be trusted, contrary to what the situation-ethics people say. Feelings are reliable only when they are based on truth and righteousness. God's people need to fill their minds with the Word of God so their feelings will correspond to God's purity. When my college friend eventually brought his thoughts "unto captivity . . . to the obedience of Christ" his feelings followed suit (2 Corinthians 10:5).

The same thing will happen to the feelings of the perennial doubter who is filled with the Spirit, but it will take time to feel consistently secure. If he looks to the Lord for mercy and forgiveness each time he feels doubtful or unbelieving, he will gradually be assured by the Lord. But if he continues to think negatively or doubtfully and justifies it by saying, "I've always been this way," he will remain that way. Or he may get worse, because he is quenching the Holy Spirit by indulging in this sin and etching the habit deeper on his mind. If he will give mental assent to such scriptural promises as Philippians 4:13, "I can do all things through Christ which strengtheneth me," he will gradually "feel" assured. Faith is taking God at his word and acting upon his promises. Anything short of that is sin, which will thwart the work of the Holy Spirit in transforming one's temperament.

Mr. Sanguine and Mr. Choleric have a similar problem with their pet sin of anger. It isn't long after they are filled with the Holy Spirit that their ingrained anger feelings rise up to grieve the Holy Spirit. Unless they immediately confess this sin, they will no longer be filled with the Spirit and the old feelings will control them. Each time they think self-righteously of how they have been offended or insulted or cheated, they cultivate feelings of hostility. These easily-triggered feelings are the result of years of hostile thoughts that can be overcome only as the Spirit of God is given access to and control of the conscious and subconscious mind. He replaces these hostile thoughts with love, kindness, and gentleness, but it will take time for a permanent change to be accomplished.

In my own case, hostility had been a way of life for thirty-six years. I sincerely wanted to be a servant of God, and I always asked for his cleansing and filling just prior to preaching, but I thought that controlling my anger was the same as victory over anger. Nothing could be further from the truth! One day, at my wife's invitation, I went to Forest Home Conference Grounds to hear Dr. Henry Brandt. I arrived just in time to hear him tell the story of an angry young minister who had come to him for counseling. It was another man, but my story! When he finished his message with Ephesians 4:30-32, I was stunned. Never had I confronted the fact that anger, hostility, and bitterness comprised an awful sin that grieved the Holy Spirit. Quietly I slunk away among the trees and poured out my heart to God. Through his mercy I was cleansed and came away a transformed man.

Facing my anger and hostility was a giant step toward true victory in my life. For the first time I really knew what it was to be filled with the Holy Spirit. Realizing the terrible nature of the sin of anger was a very humbling experience, and I was emotionally subdued for the first time in decades. But how long did the feeling last? About two hours after I left Forest Home that wonderful feeling of peace and oneness with God was drowned in the tidal waves of my habitual hostility.

One of my pet "gripes" in life was the character who suddenly cuts you off on the freeway, and many a bitter, hateful word had shot from my tongue in response to such careless driving. It happened again on my way home.

There, while traveling at 65 mph on the freeway toward San Diego, I encountered another life-changing experience. While glaring at the offending driver, I suddenly became aware that my "peace with God" had vanished. Right then, I decided he was not going to determine my spiritual failure. While reducing my speed to avoid a collision, I silently prayed, "Lord, I did it again; please forgive me and take this habit away." Gradually the "peace" came back, and this Choleric-Sanguine started out on the most exciting and satisfying period of his life.

Yes, there have been other times and other failures, but whenever I confess my anger God in his grace forgives. Now it is almost a thing of the past. Some of the things that used to "set me off" now make me laugh. Recently, while thinking about the old reactions, I found myself chuckling after being cut off on the freeway by a little red sports car. I wouldn't trade my present peace and joy for the old anger and misery under any circumstances. Incidentally, there must be something convincing about the transforming work of the Holy Spirit in my life, because the last time we had dinner with Dr. and Mrs. Brandt I overheard my wife say to him, "I want to thank you for being the vessel God used to give me a new husband." At the risk of being too personal, I might also add that had it not been for those two life-changing experiences with the Holy Spirit, I could not have produced the book entitled *How To Be Happy Though Married.*

Lest you think this kind of victory is a gift which God bestows only on ministers, I relate the story of a California highway patrolman. A strong Choleric, this young Christian had been introduced to the Spirit-filled life and was beginning to experience victory over the anger and hostility that had long controlled him. Then he had to give a ticket to a man he described as "the nastiest motorist I have ever met." The only person that was nastier, he said, was the motorist's wife. He described the experience this way. "While I wrote up their ticket, they called me every filthy word I had ever heard and some that were new. I was polite to them, as the department has instructed us, but when I got back in my car I was so mad that my face was hot and the hair on the back of my neck felt like it was standing straight out. Then I remembered about grieving the Holy Spirit. As they drove away, I bowed over my steering wheel and confessed my sin, asking God to forgive them and lead someone into their lives to save them. As I looked up, they were almost out of sight down the highway, and I was conscious of a deep feeling of peace and love. All the bitterness was gone. I started my engine and drove on to enjoy a good day instead of the miserable day I would ordinarily have had." He went on to tell how he had the joy that night of leading an accident victim to a saving knowledge of Christ. This proves again the Holy Spirit is in the business of transforming human temperament.

How to walk in the Spirit

Many books have been written on how to be filled with the Spirit, but most have not given sufficient emphasis to the fact that being filled with the Spirit is just the beginning of Christian victory. From that point on we must "walk in the Spirit" to be lastingly effective (Galatians 5:16). It is one thing to start out in the Spirit-filled life and quite another to walk day by day in the control of the Spirit. Just as we are commanded to "be filled with the Spirit," we are instructed to "walk in the Spirit." Since it is a command of God, we must not search for a hard or complex procedure, for God is straightening out our lives, not tangling them up. The following procedure for walking in the Spirit can be a practical tool for victorious daily living.

1. *Make the filling of the Holy Spirit a daily priority.* You cannot walk in the Spirit unless you sincerely want to and unless you have his filling. As we have already seen, old habit patterns sneak back to haunt us. If we enjoy them more than the peace of God, we will indulge the sins of the flesh. Let's be honest: lust, worry, self-pity, and anger are fun — temporarily. The aftermath is miserable. Only when we consciously and subconsciously want the filling of the Holy Spirit more than anything else in the world are we willing to give up our lesser emotional satisfactions of lust, worry, self-pity, and anger.

I confess that even after several years of experiencing the Holy Spirit's filling, I find that anger is fun. Under certain circumstances, such as when I feel my "rights have been violated," I can anticipate a satisfying bout with anger. However, the Spirit's reminder of the high price I must pay for indulging such an emotion cools me off immediately. No cause for anger is worth the loss of that blessed consciousness of his presence. Gradually the reaction becomes subconscious so that you can begin to say with Paul, "The things I once loved I now hate."

A good spiritual exercise in this connection is to make a list of the kind of person you would most like to be. Such a list would include some of the following:

1. a Christlike Christian doing God's "perfect will";
2. a fruitful Christian laying up treasures in heaven;
3. an unselfish, loving partner;
4. a successful parent whose children follow Christ;
5. an effective Christian worker in the local church;
6. a capable, productive employee or housewife;
7. a good neighbor.

Your enjoyment of life depends primarily on the attainment of spiritual goals, not on fame, fortune, food, and fun, the objectives of worldly people and apparently of many Christians. The question you should answer is this: how many of these lifetime priorities can you fulfill without the Holy Spirit? The answer is: not one! When this truth really grips your mind and heart, you will be well on the road to walking in the Spirit. Just as a young mother is so sensitive to her sleeping infant's needs that she awakens at his slightest movement, so the Spirit-filled Christian subconsciously responds to the Holy Spirit. The mother — and the Christian — respond intuitively to their number one priority.

2. Develop a keen sensitivity to sin. As we have already seen, sin short-circuits the power of the Holy Spirit in us. The moment we are conscious of any sins of the mind, we should confess them immediately; in this way the time between grieving or quenching the Spirit and reinstatement is minimal. The main advantage to the study of temperaments is that we can diagnose our most common weakness. Consequently, we are on our guard for "the sin that doth so easily beset us." When it rears its ugly head, confess it, forget it (God does, so you might as well), and press on toward the fulfillment of the will of God for your life. The main secret to victorious living among those I have counseled has been the practice of instant confession.

3. Daily read and study God's Word. It is my conviction after a good deal of observation that it is impossible for a Christian to "walk in the Spirit" unless he develops the habit of regularly feeding his mind and heart upon the Word of

God. One of the reasons Christians do not "feel" as God does about life issues is they do not know God's way from his Word.

Since our feelings are produced by our thought processes, we will feel as carnal wordlings do if we feed our minds on the "wisdom of the world." If we feed our minds on the Word of God, we will feel as the Spirit does about life issues. Remember that it takes some time to reorient our minds from human wisdom to divine wisdom. So regular reading is essential.

Sometimes Christians object that this will make them legalists or bring them into bondage to a mental habit. Yet they don't seem to view coming to the table three times a day as legalistic. We do it because we sense a need and enjoy eating. In the same way, we can feed spiritually on God's Word from a sense of need, but it takes time to build our spiritual appetite. Many Christians feel something is wrong if they miss reading the Word of God, but they didn't start out that way. It takes self-discipline to develop good habits of thinking, but once established they become "second nature."

Several years ago I challenged a Sunday school class to the daily reading of one chapter in the book of Proverbs. There are thirty-one chapters in Proverbs, so I suggested they read whatever chapter matched the day of the month. One year later a successful businessman commented, "When you gave that challenge, I wasn't convinced it would work, but I have been doing it every day this year and consider it the primary reason I am a consistent Christian for the first time." This man went from being an average church member who occasionally shared his faith to a dynamic and bold witness with outstanding success. The daily feeding on the Word gave him a calm assurance plus the wisdom of God to share with others.

A young engineer came to me after eleven years as a Christian and confessed he had never led a person to Christ. Moreover, he claimed: "I never get an opportunity to witness my faith." But after three months of a consistent Bible reading and memorization program, he told me with a big smile: "That was nonsense about never having an opportunity to witness. I witness all the time now. I previously knew so little about the Bible that I didn't have anything to say, but now that I'm so full of the Word it comes out in almost every conversation!"

A consistent feeding of one's mind upon the Word of God produces some interesting results. Consider the following revolutionary benefits:

Joshua 1:8 — It makes your way prosperous and gives success.
Psalm 1:3 — It produces fruitfulness and
Psalm 119:11 — It keeps us from sin.
John 14:21 — God reveals himself increasingly to keepers of his Word.
John 15:3 — The Word cleanses us.
John 15:7 — The Word produces power in prayer.
John 15:11 — The Word brings joy to our hearts.
1 John 2:13, 14 — The Word gives victory over "the wicked one."

With these transforming results from filling our minds with God's Word, it is a tragedy that so many Christians live a second-rate life with feelings of insecurity, uncleanness, discontent, anxiety, and impotence. The character of our feelings depends on the character of our thoughts, and the sincere Christian should ask himself: What is shaping and filling my thoughts? The answer will describe your feelings that permeate, surround, and motivate you every day.

A careful comparison of the Spirit-filled life described in Ephesians 5:18-21 with the Word-filled life in Colossians 3: 15-17 is very revealing. Both passages promise: a song in your heart, a thanksgiving attitude, and a submissive spirit. A mind that is filled with and yielded to the Word of God will produce the same effects on our emotions as the mind filled with and yielded to the Holy Spirit. We may legitimately conclude from this that the filling of the Spirit and walking in the Spirit depend upon our filling with the Word of God!

Through the years I have developed habits to renew my

mind — and thereby my feelings — toward God. These habits are night Bible reading and meditation. Reading the Bible at night makes the subconscious mind work for us while the body is sleeping. The mind digests the events and thoughts of the day, particularly the last things we think about before going to sleep. For that reason it is very profitable to read God's Word just before retiring and go to sleep thinking about the things just read. It is amazing how this helps me to awaken with a positive outlook for the day. If you can read in bed, all the better. Get into the habit of reading the Word just before sleeping, and your subconscious mind will mold your feelings in God's patterns.

The other valuable habit is meditation. To me that simply means "thinking." The mind is always working, and our will determines whether our mind works for or against us. To work for good, the mind must meditate on the truths and insights of God's Word. There is one catch: you must memorize in order to meditate profitably, because you can't meditate on what you don't know intimately. Whether it is a phrase, concept, or whole verse of Scripture, you must memorize it in order to meditate on it. Otherwise, you can meditate only when you have an open Bible before you.

A simple method I use to inspire meditation is to write special verses that bless my soul on a sheet of paper in my Bible or notebook. I learn at least one of these verses every week. It is hard work, but most of us use less than 10 percent of our brain potential! And as you force yourself to hide God's Word in your heart, you improve your memory for other things. I don't know any mentally lazy Christians who walk in the Spirit. And Spirit-filled Christians are the most mentally stimulating people I meet.

4. Guard against grieving the Holy Spirit. The next step for walking in the Spirit is an extension of step two — developing a sensitivity to sin. Ephesians 4:30-32 makes it clear that all forms of hostility, including anger, bitterness, and enmity, grieve the Holy Spirit. All anger-prone believers should memorize those three verses and develop a particular sensitivity to hostility. In addition to making instant confession, they should resolve to be loving, kind, tenderhearted, and forgiving toward others. This grace is markedly unnatural for a Sanguine or a Choleric, but the Holy Spirit will develop in the believer a new capacity for thoughtfulness and love.

This supernaturally induced love is mentally and emotionally healthful as well as spiritually rejuvenating. I counseled two strongwilled men who were maliciously persecuted by their employers. One was fired after he refused to quit under pressure. His Spirit-filled reaction was to lead his family in praying for his employer. This earned him the special admiration of his wife, children, and friends, and he found another job where he contentedly awaits God's further will for his life.

The second man suffered an emotional breakdown from the stress and came to see me a few days after he was released from the psychiatric department of a local hospital. Never had I seen more vehement hatred. The selfishness and brutality of the former employer was still fresh to him, and he would not forgive the offender.

If only he realized the high cost of harboring such hatred, he would forgive the man. Since he grieved the Spirit long ago, he knows nothing about the Spirit-filled life and his hostility is destroying him. Functioning on his own, his mind is playing tricks on him: he is imagining that his wife is unfaithful and his children don't love him, and more recently he concluded that even his parents do not love him. All of this abnormal behavior is the perfectly natural result of long-harbored hatred. Christians are admonished to "forgive one another," not only for God's glory and the offender's good, but for the offended one's peace of mind. When you prize the filling of the Holy Spirit above everything else, you won't let anger, animosity, or unforgiveness grieve the Holy Spirit. You know you can't afford it!

Several years ago I counseled with a couple who had been separated because of the husband's infidelity. He finally repented toward God and his wife and she decided to take him back. Their home was reestablished on a spiritual foundation, but within a month the wife was back in my office in tears. "I hate my husband and can't bear to have him touch me!" she sobbed. Prior to his unfaithfulness she had dearly loved him, I knew. After asking God for wisdom, I inquired if she had forgiven her husband for what he had done. She sat up straight and fire blazed in her eyes. "Why should I? He doesn't deserve to be forgiven! As a Christian he knew better than that!"

All of this was true, of course. As gently as possible I showed her that none of us deserves forgiveness, yet God commands us to forgive one another even as he forgives us. When she realized she didn't want to forgive her husband and this grieved the Holy Spirit, she began to pray. Forgetting her husband's sin, she began to concentrate on her own sins of resentment, hatred, and lack of forgiveness. She got up from her knees a transformed woman. Today she is a Spirit-filled, radiant Christian who joyfully loves her husband — certainly a rich reward for obediently forgiving one who didn't deserve forgiveness!

The importance of our will becomes apparent at this point of walking in the Spirit. When we feel the bludgeon of injustice or someone's wrath, we are forced either to hate the offender or to forgive and pray for him. Our overall feelings as well as our walk in the Spirit depend upon our decision. Don't be surprised if you fail repeatedly at first. Only be sure that you confess the sin as soon as you are aware of grieving the Spirit, and let him reestablish your walk. As you choose to forgive and to let the Holy Spirit react with patience and love, you will find your temperament weakness changing into a strength.

5. *Avoid quenching the Spirit through fear and worry.* According to 1 Thessalonians 5:16-19, we quench the Holy Spirit when we doubt and resist his dealings in our lives. When a Christian says, "I don't understand why God let this awful thing happen to me," he has already quenched the Spirit through fear and is no longer walking in the Spirit. The Christian who is trusting God could face the same circumstances

and say, "I thank God he is in control of my life! I don't understand his dealings with me right now, but I trust his promise that he will never leave me and he will supply my every need." Such a Christian continues to walk in the Spirit and "feels good" in spite of adverse circumstances.

We have seen that melancholy and phlegmatic people have a predisposition toward fear, just as the more extrovertive temperaments have a predisposition toward anger. Some people possess both introvertive and extrovertive temperaments, and consequently may have deep problems with both fear and anger. God's grace is sufficient to cure both problems through his Holy Spirit. But if you have these tendencies, you need to watch carefully your reaction to seemingly unfavorable events. If you groan or complain inwardly, you have already quenched the Holy Spirit. This can be remedied immediately if you are willing to call your doubt-induced complaining exactly what it is — *sin* — and ask God to transform this habit pattern and fill you with his Spirit.

Frequently I meet people who say, "I tried that, but it didn't work." What they may have tried is to escape an undesirable problem or difficulty, through confession of their complaining, rather than accepting the problem and thanking God for it.

God is not nearly so interested in changing circumstances as he is in changing people. It is no victory to live without worry when there is nothing to worry about. Victory comes when we face a worrisome problem and do not worry. Becoming a Christian did not exempt you from trouble. Job said, "Yet man is born unto trouble, as the sparks fly upward" (Job 5: 7). Jesus warned us we would face tribulation in this world, and the Bible tells us God sends testings to strengthen us. Many Christians flunk the tests by seeking their removal rather than rendering obedience in the Spirit.

It is impossible for a fear-prone Christian to walk in the Spirit any length of time without strong infusions of God's Word to encourage his faith. The more God's Word fills his mind, the more his feelings abound in faith. But worriers usually enjoy wallowing in their misery, especially with God watching the piteous scene. Prayer for such people often makes them feel worse. As they whine in prayer, they stamp their misfortunes more deeply on their minds and feel worse at the end of their prayer than when they started. That does not mean prayer is bad; it means the wrong kind of prayer is bad. We must go to God's Word to see what constitutes beneficial prayer.

All worriers should memorize Philippians 4:6-7, "Be careful for nothing; but in everything by prayer and supplication with thanksgiving let your requests be made known unto God. And the peace of God, which passeth all understanding, shall keep your hearts and minds through Christ Jesus." These verses direct prayer to be made "with thanksgiving." You cannot genuinely pray with thanksgiving and finish with the same burdens you started with. Consider the following two prayers — and the emotions they create — offered by Christian parents with a sick child.

"Dear Lord, we come to you on behalf of our little girl so near death. The doctor tells us there is no hope for her. Please, dear Lord, heal her. You know how much she means to us. If this sickness is caused by sin in our lives, forgive and cleanse us that she may live. After all the other tragedies in our lives, we do not think we can bear another. In Jesus' name. Amen."

"Dear heavenly Father, thank you that we are your children and can look to you at this time of need. You know the report of the doctors and you have promised that all things work together for good to folks like us. We don't understand our dear child's sickness, but we know you love us and are more than able to heal her. We commit her little body to you, Father, asking for her healing according to your perfect will. We dedicated her to you before she was born, and we thank you that you are able to supply all her needs, right now, as well as ours. In Jesus' name. Amen."

It is obvious which set of parents will feel the "peace of God" and which couple will wring their hands in anguish at this time of deep need. The difference comes in learning the attitude of thanksgiving from the Word of God. Lest you think the above prayer is hypothetical or idealistic, let me share a personal experience. The blonde, blue-eyed cutie named Lori that God sent to us is the apple of my heart. Five years ago I stood at her bedside in Children's Hospital and prayed that prayer. Frankly, I don't know how people without Jesus Christ go through such trials. My wife and I can testify that in spite of Lori's raging fever and delirium, and no known hope, God imparted peace to our troubled hearts. However, not until we prayed with thanksgiving beside her oxygen tent did we receive that peace.

If you tend to worry or grumble, you will find that you are not a very thankful person. You may be a fine person in many other respects, but unless you learn to be thankful you can never walk far in the Spirit, nor will you be a consistently happy person. The secret to a thanksgiving attitude is in coming to know God intimately as he reveals himself in his Word. This will require consistent Bible reading, studying, and meditation. When your faith is established through the Word, it is easier to give thanks but it is still an act of the will. If you have not accepted his full leading for your life, you will complain because you doubt things will turn out all right. And doubt quenches the Spirit and sidetracks your real progress.

Several months ago I experienced the most devastating emotional trauma that had entered my life since my father died thirty-four years ago. For almost three years I had worked on a project desperately needed by our church — new property. After much prayer and work, our people caught the vision to trust God for the impossible. We purchased forty-three acres of ground near two freeways at an approximate cost of $500,000. We considered it the most strategic location in our city for a growing church. I had eaten, slept, prayed, and lived that project during these three years. In fact, this book would have been out a year earlier had I not spent so much time on the project.

Somehow local politics got involved, and some of the city fathers began to oppose the zone change we needed to build

on our property. For two years we carried on a running battle with city hall. We spent thousands of dollars on lawyers'
and engineers' fees plus an equal number of man-hours.
Through all that time there was absolutely no doubt in my
mind that the plans would be approved and we would build a
beautiful church to God's glory. Then on October 7, 1969, after hours of deliberation, the city council voted 6 to 2 *against*
us. I was so stunned I couldn't get up out of my chair at
first. Eventually I mustered enough strength to leave as dis-
creetly as possible.

When I finally got away from everyone, I drove alone to the
property. I didn't have the courage to visit the spot where my
wife and I had knelt and claimed that property for God. Instead, I went out to a lovely vantage point and sat down in
the dirt to think. Can you imagine the nature of my first
thoughts? I must confess they weren't very pleasant. "Why,
Lord? Why did you let this happen? What did I do wrong?
I prayed over this place, I walked over it and claimed it, just
as others did for theirs. Why did you let this happen? It
worked for Abraham, for some of my minister friends; why
hasn't it worked for me? Why did you let a selfish politician
who didn't want a church next to his house disgrace your good
name and that of our church?"

I had lots of questions. And the more I griped, the worse
I felt. About that time the opposing politician drove into his
driveway. I watched from my spot of self-pity across the can-
yon from his house as he got out of his big Lincoln Conti-
nental and presented his wife with a basket of flowers to cele-
brate his victory. Guess how I felt! Absolutely miserable.
I was even tempted to ask God to knock those flowers out of
his hand with a bolt of lightning, but the Lord squelched that
temptation.

For two days I went through the worst siege of depression
I have ever experienced. Finally it dawned on me that I had
quenched the Holy Spirit and was walking in a very carnal
state. The thought came to me, "Here you are, the author of a
book with a chapter on how to cure depression, a preacher

who challenges Christians not to become depressed — and *you* are depressed. Why don't you practice what you preach?" After confessing my sins of self-pity, doubt, griping, and questioning God, I began thanking him. I thanked him for his power and leading, and that though I didn't know what he was going to do, the problem wasn't really mine but his.

A thrilling thing happened that day. The depression lifted, my spirit began to rise, and a deep peace flooded my heart. During succeeding months, though actively engaged in the search for new property and knocking on every door of opportunity, I gained no more idea of God's plan for our church than I had had on October 7. The thrilling part, however, is that I have not felt the slightest twinge of discouragement. Our people have responded in such faith that we are convinced God has something better for us than we had planned before. Only God can produce joy and peace in the face of seeming chaos. The good feelings, however, didn't start until the servant began thanking God by faith. There is a mysterious therapy in thanksgiving; it invokes the emotional ministrations of the Holy Spirit. His peace remains, though the problem is still unsettled.

This valuable lesson points out that there are two kinds of thanks. The first kind is natural and easy when we are walking by sight: we know where we are going and the prospects are pleasant. The second is supernatural and is by faith: we cannot see what God is doing or why, but we are thankful he is leading, and he will never forsake us. That kind of thanksgiving comes while walking in the Spirit.

Our hymnal contains the gospel song "Count Your Many Blessings." Note these words:

Count your many blessings,
Name them one by one,
And it will surprise you
What the Lord has done.

Many Christians aren't aware what God has done for them because they haven't started to count their blessings.

Have you counted yours lately? These riches increase with the counting!

One last practical suggestion for walking in the Spirit is in order here. Although mental attitude is important at all times, it is of paramount importance twice during each day: when we go to bed, and when we arise. It is very important to pray "with thanksgiving" and "in everything give thanks" as well as reading the Scriptures at night. Though it may be hard, the other strategic time to give thanks is the first thing in the morning.

A neurosurgeon in Atlanta says, "The most important period of your day is the first thirty minutes after you wake up. What you think during that time sets the pattern for your emotional attitude all day." This would be particularly true of "early birds," folks who get drowsy in the evening but awaken bright-eyed and refreshed in the morning. Nocturnalists, by contrast, are generally not very sharp the first thing in the morning. In any case, the doctor's statement points up the importance of prayer with thanksgiving to start the day. The Psalmist helps us: "This is the day which the Lord hath made; we will rejoice and be glad in it" (Psalm 118:24).

After beginning your day with thanksgiving, yield yourself anew to God according to Romans 6:11-13. Tell him you are available to share your faith with the needy one he sends to you. Yield your lips to the Holy Spirit and let him open the conversation. Walk in the Spirit and you will bear fruit for God. As soon as you sense you have grieved or quenched the Spirit, confess your sin and again ask for his filling. If you follow these steps, your temperament will truly be transformed!